THE FINEST
MENSWEAR
IN THE WORLD

Simon Crompton

THE FINEST
MENSWEAR
IN THE WORLD

THE CRAFTSMANSHIP OF LUXURY

350 illustrations

Thames & Hudson

PRECEDING PAGE: The author wearing a Cifonelli
suit, a Kiton shirt and a Begg & Co. scarf.

First published in 2016 in hardcover in the United States of America by
Thames & Hudson Inc., 500 Fifth Avenue, New York, New York 10110

thamesandhudsonusa.com

Library of Congress Catalog Card Number 2015941297

ISBN 978-0-500-51809-0

Designed by Adam Hay Studio

Printed and bound in China by C&C Offset Printing Co. Ltd

CONTENTS

INTRODUCTION
THE CRAFT BEHIND THE FINEST MENSWEAR IN THE WORLD

Baby cashmere is only two microns finer than regular cashmere, but ten years and millions of dollars were spent convincing Mongolian herdsmen to gather it. To sew a Milanese buttonhole, a tailor must spend almost an hour carefully winding silk for something only an aficionado will see. These are tiny details – in the eyes of many, needless details – but they are what elevate a fine piece of menswear into being the finest of its kind.

I remember the first time I saw a bespoke suit being made. I was simply staggered at the level of craft. The chest of the suit is constructed from layers of horsehair, canvas and felt, sewn together with hundreds of hand stitches. The top of the sleeve is much bigger than the armhole it goes into and must be worked in stitch by stitch. Even a patch pocket is a work of art. Some of these crafts produce beauty – such as the Milanese buttonholes. Others create greater comfort – such as the sleeve/armhole combination. Still others are questions of innovation and perseverance, such as the baby cashmere. But they all have the same aim: to achieve the highest possible quality.

A fading beauty

This excellence in menswear has become harder to discern. Thirty years ago, it was remarked that for the first time people were wearing labels on the outside of their clothes. Since then, branding has become all-powerful. Men, even more than women, have adopted brands as a shorthand for quality and style. Faced with an indigestible number of choices, they retreat to the safety of a familiar name.

Advertising and the 'communications' industry don't help. Often, they deliberately obfuscate. Old brands will play on their longevity, while local brands emphasize nationality, even though neither necessarily has anything to do with quality. Combine that with ill-trained sales staff and the rise of internet shopping, and understanding quality in menswear has never been harder.

This book is hopefully a step in the right direction. By explaining how the finest clothes are made it aims to deepen understanding and lead to more discerning choices. I make no argument with men who have simply given up on clothing. As Bruce Boyer, one of the greatest menswear writers, put it, they did not reason their way into their position and they will not be reasoned out of it. This book is addressed, rather, to men who want to be able to turn aside one brand in favour of another, confident in its inherent quality – who want to be able to select the finest menswear in the world.

The methodology

Judgments of what constitutes the 'best' in any field are subjective, simply because no judge uses the same criteria. But a discussion of the finest can be different. A judgment on the finest wool thread is objective. So too the length of yarn. The products recommended in this book are, in that sense, the finest available anywhere in the world. They use the best materials and they require the most skill and time to make: they are the zenith of their art.

One or two points remain subjective – and where so, this will be clearly admitted. The fineness of a Drake's tie, for example, is down to both technical aspects, such as the hand-screen printing of silk, and aesthetic points, such as the sophistication of the designs. Some of the information in the following chapters is also rather technical. That is deliberate. The intention throughout is to help those with the money and desire for the finest menswear in the world but a paucity of information.

The judgments and selections are my own, and are based on wide-ranging experience in the luxury industry. For every factory mentioned, chances are I've also visited most of their main competitors. I own every product, and have tried and reviewed many others. Most importantly, I have made use of extensive contacts among manufacturers, agents and buyers to validate my conclusions.

To qualify for inclusion in this book, companies have to design, make and sell their own product, and thereby control its quality throughout. There are some great factories out there, maintaining the highest standards of traditional manufacturing, but their product is rebranded by a variety of designers and their recommendation is therefore complicated.

Equally, some brands should be applauded for seeking out the best factories in Europe and even China to make their menswear. But their control of the process is never complete, and production policies change.

One result of emphasizing both the manufacturing and retail sides of the industry is that all the items recommended in this book can be readily purchased, although sometimes this requires a trip to England or Italy, and perhaps a six-month wait. Each will more than reward the time spent learning about them, and any travel or delay: their careful and steady acquisition will give any man a peerless modern wardrobe.

BIOGRAPHY

THE CONNOISSEUR BEHIND THE FINEST MENSWEAR IN THE WORLD

Simon Crompton is one of the world's leading authorities on luxury menswear, with a particular passion for bespoke tailoring and traditional crafts. An author and journalist, he is sought after by publications such as *How to Spend It* and the *Telegraph* for both his advice on modern men's style and his expertise in handmade clothing, its values and quality.

Over the past ten years Simon has built up an enthusiastic fan base through his online magazine Permanent Style, which has been listed as one of the best in the world by both *The Times* and the *New York Times*. In a world crowded with amateur bloggers, Permanent Style is noted for its eloquence, erudition and industry-insider access.

In recent years Permanent Style has evolved into a platform for events, clothing collaborations and publishing, with a yearly hard-copy annual.

Educated at Trinity College, Oxford, Simon trained as a financial journalist before turning his attention to menswear. He lives in Peckham in south London with his wife and two daughters.

ANDERSON & SHEPPARD

THE FINEST SPORTS JACKETS
IN THE WORLD

DISTINCTIVE DRAPE

ANDERSON & SHEPPARD COMBINE THE
FINESSE OF SAVILE ROW TAILORING WITH
A DISTINCTIVE CUT THAT USES EXCESS
MATERIAL TO FLATTER THE FIGURE.

You can have many things made bespoke: shoes, briefcases, seven-fold ties. But nothing makes a greater difference to how you look and feel than a bespoke jacket. Men's upper bodies vary a lot. Yes, many look good in a 38R, but if you really want to fit a jacket to a man's shape you need to consider many other dimensions. Everyone leans slightly to one side, for instance, and everyone stoops a bit. Even the rotation of our torso varies, so our arms fall differently. It may only be a matter of a quarter of an inch, but adding these asymmetries together results in a complex three-dimensional map. A bespoke jacket, which will fit well, cannot help but make you look more confident, more composed and more athletic.

Everyone used to have bespoke suits. Tailors, catering to different income levels, could be found all over London. The less expensive tailors used a sewing machine to make most of their products, but they were still cut and fitted by hand – creating that same enviable bespoke fit. Realizing there were economies of scale, some tailors created chains of stores. By 1945 over 60% of men in the UK were dressed by just two houses – Burton and Hepworth. The bespoke cutting was only lost in the 1950s and 1960s when mass manufacturing made ready-to-wear suits the norm.

Today, most of the bespoke cutting that has survived is at the high end of the market, based around Savile Row. They marry the hand-cutting with

ABOVE: Tailor's chalk, used to mark both cloth and paper patterns; fittings hanging in the Anderson & Sheppard workroom.

OPPOSITE: A customer's jacket begins life as a set of paper patterns, which will be used as templates to cut the cloth.

FOLLOWING PAGES: Paper patterns hang up waiting to be used; head cutter John Hitchcock uses the patterns to cut the panels of a suit.

ABOVE: A tailor works on part of a basted fitting. Loose, long stitches are used to roughly hold the parts of the suit together.

OPPOSITE: Fundamental to the art of a bespoke suit is the hand padding of the chest, which creates shapes not possible with a machine-made garment. Anderson & Sheppard uses longer stitches than most English tailors, leading to a softer chest.

hand-sewing, creating beautiful jackets that have graced the backs of royalty, aristocracy and, latterly, stars in the world of entertainment. For my money, the maker of the finest sports jackets in the world is Anderson & Sheppard, the tailor of choice for many in the entertainment business during the 20th century.

A more perfect make

A Savile Row suit is made almost entirely by hand, which makes it a finer product and increases its longevity – both nice things to have. Far more important, however, are the elements of handwork that will make a suit more comfortable and a better fit.

I began by describing the three-dimensional nature of a man's torso. Let's explain how tailoring by hand makes a suit fit more perfectly to that torso. In the chest of a suit are three layers of material that make up its 'canvas'. These are horsehair, canvas and domette (a kind of felt). They are stitched together by hand, usually across the tailor's knee. The size of the stitches varies from tailor to tailor, and gives their suits a subtly different character: smaller stitches produce a firmer, more solid structure, while larger ones lead to a softer, more malleable feel. The weight of the canvas materials also varies.

All of these jackets have one thing in common: this structured, handmade canvas will form the shape of the chest, moulding to it and so making a better-fitting jacket. It creates a three-dimensional shape. In a traditional English suit, the canvas will also stretch all the way down the front of the jacket, giving the lower half greater structure. Handmade shoulder pads achieve something similar with their layers of soft wadding. An Anderson & Sheppard jacket has all of this and more. Most tailors, for example, position the canvas

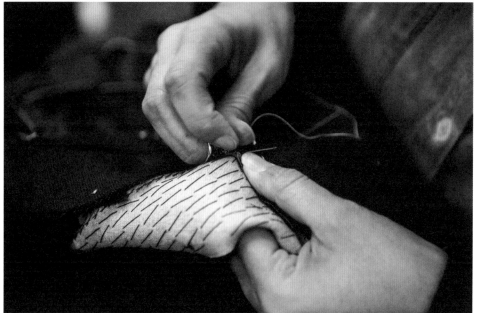

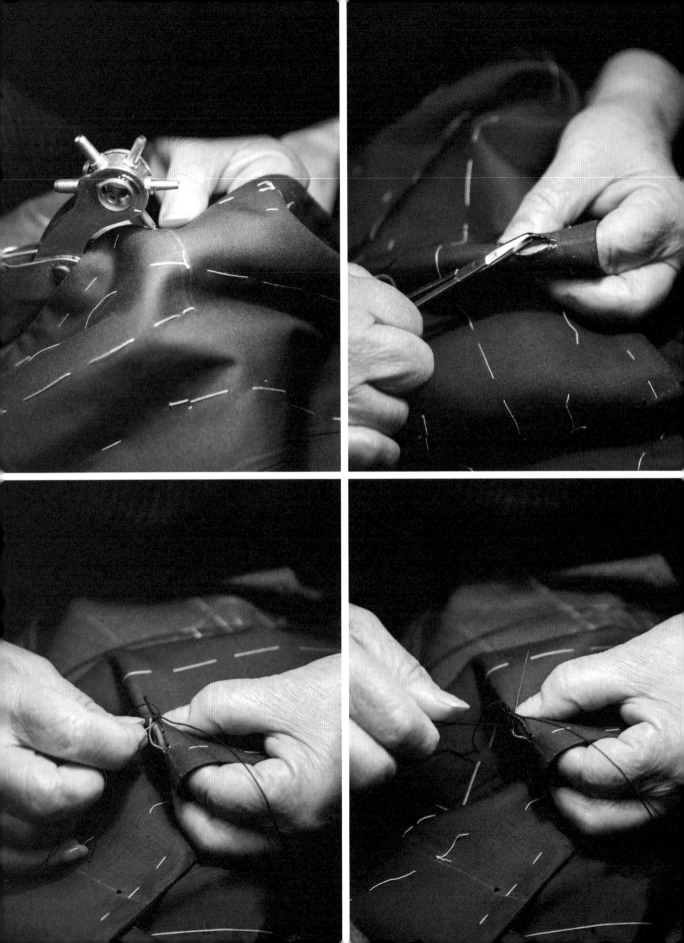

so that its weave is at right angles to the suit. This makes it stronger, firmer and more rigid. But with an Anderson & Sheppard jacket, the canvas is cut at a slight angle (around 30 degrees), which means it can stretch. The chest becomes more lissom and lithe.

The jacket is also lent flexibility by the stitching along its shoulder seam. Even some of the most expensive tailors prefer to sew this part by machine, either because it is easier or because they believe it produces a cleaner line. Anderson & Sheppard sews the shoulder by hand, so there is greater movement in the seam. If you have the chance, pick up a jacket and, while holding the shoulder in one hand and the collar in the other, try to stretch the seam. It is surprising how rigid the line is when it has been machine sewn and, in contrast, how flexible it is if sewn by hand. The Anderson & Sheppard seam also slopes slightly backwards, permitting more movement in the shoulder and arm.

The perfect accompaniment to this pliable shoulder is a sleeve sewn onto the jacket by hand. This enables the jacket to have a small armhole and a larger sleeve, with the latter eased into the former gradually, working in the excess cloth. The great advantage of a large sleevehead and a small armhole is that it allows the arm to move freely without dragging the rest of the suit with it.

This may seem a little counter-intuitive: surely a larger armhole would permit more movement. There is certainly space, but pulling in the rest of the jacket makes the waist, neck and opposing arm uncomfortable, all for the sake of a little breathing room. A small armhole isolates the arm, allowing it to move independently.

All Savile Row tailors and some designer brands attach the sleeve by hand. Anderson & Sheppard, however, uses a bit more cloth in the sleeve, exaggerating the effect in order to achieve greater comfort. Tailors from Naples often use the same size of sleevehead, but they work more of it in at the top of the shoulder, showing off the technique by leaving the excess cloth to ripple down the sleeve. Anderson & Sheppard prefers a more subtle style. In this way its jackets are a perfect midpoint between the two most distinctive traditions in bespoke tailoring: the lightweight Neapolitan and the structured English military.

ABOVE: A sewing machine is still used for some aspects of the suit where there is no advantage to handwork, particularly with long, straight seams.

OPPOSITE: To the discerning eye, a hand-sewn buttonhole is an indicator of a bespoke suit. It involves careful, painstaking work.

ABOVE AND OPPOSITE: Waistcoats and suits await customers downstairs at the Old Burlington Street shop.

If you would like to see the construction method for yourself, pop along to the Anderson & Sheppard shop on Old Burlington Street, just behind Savile Row. The front-of-house staff are always willing to offer a demonstration of its beneficial effects.

The drape

The last distinctive aspect of Anderson & Sheppard tailoring deserves some historical context. The firm was established in 1906 when Per Anderson, the founder, was trained by the legendary creator of the drape cut, Dutchman Frederick Scholte. He found that by adding extra material in the chest and back of a jacket, while still bringing it in tight at the waist, he could create the impression of a powerful physique and make the suit more comfortable.

This method of draping cloth from broad shoulder to narrow waist was revolutionary. In 1949 Scholte's obituary in the magazine *Tailor & Cutter* said it was 'one of the greatest changes in men's fashion that has ever been introduced'. The movement of that draped chest is also helped by Anderson & Sheppard's soft canvas, cut on the bias.

There are echoes here of the evolution of the suit itself, for the change in men's clothing between the 17th and 19th centuries can be seen as a shift from drape to fit, from longer, flowing silks to tight-fitting wools. There were many advantages to the emphasis on fit, not least the fact that it gave birth to the technical art of tailoring and England's domination of it. But anyone with more than a passing interest in fashion will appreciate that drape and cut are just as important in achieving a flattering look. The key is to let the cloth work with you.

Catering to men of style

The skill with which Anderson & Sheppard cutters have consistently executed their drape and cut technique is the reason the house has survived for over 100 years. And because many of the visitors to their shop – the great, the good and, perhaps more importantly, the stylish – have become loyal customers.

We know they had style because many of them were entertainers whose image has been fixed on film. Among early English supporters were Noël Coward, Herbert Marshall and Cary Grant. There were also a few Americans who spent their days acting as if they were British – Fred Astaire and Gary Cooper – plus stately stars Douglas Fairbanks and Jack Buchanan.

Once fitted with the Anderson & Sheppard drape, stars became not just converts but evangelists. Anderson & Sheppard's 'day books' show that Astaire, Coward and twenties icon Clifton Webb each recommended over 20 men to the firm. A reference was usually given for a new customer, so this network of recommendations and enthusiastic word of mouth is evident year after year. George Gershwin recommended his brother Ira; Richard Rodgers put in for his songwriting partner Lorenz Hart. The list, including Cole Porter, Rudolph Valentino, Charlie Chaplin and Marlene Dietrich, goes on.

Anderson & Sheppard always had a reputation for being discreet, even secretive. This attitude has softened over the years, and today it is one of the more open and progressive of the Savile Row houses. Partially as a result, a new generation of customers is breathing its air of quiet refinement, and recommending to each other the commissioning of perhaps the finest jacket in the world.

RIGHT: The 'day books' at Anderson & Sheppard contain entries for many famous men of the 20th century, particularly show business stars such as Fred Astaire and Gary Cooper.

BEGG & CO.

THE FINEST SCARVES
IN THE WORLD

A SCOTTISH SOFTIE

BEGG IS THE ONLY LUXURY WEAVER
ENTIRELY DEDICATED TO SCARVES.
LATELY, THAT DEDICATION HAS
GENERATED BOTH STRONG DESIGN
AND TECHNICAL INNOVATION.

The location of scarf-maker Begg, on Scotland's south-west coast, is not the most inviting. The factory sits on a side street, opposite blocks of housing in various stages of disrepair. It is in the town of Ayr, which faces out onto the Firth of Clyde and across the wind-whipped sea to Arran. It is not, to put it lightly, an environment one would associate with luxurious, diaphanous cashmere.

Indeed, the factory shop would likely sell out in minutes if it was located in a little side street in Mayfair. The £240 scarves are reduced to £60 all year round, yet there is no stampede of locals every time a new batch is released from the factory. Instead, two staff oversee a calm little shop filled with shelf upon shelf of the ultimate in women's and men's neckwear.

There is a similar contrast inside the factory between the hulking, frenetic looms and the finished items, which are carefully pressed and wrapped in tissue paper at the other end of the line. It is a contrast you often see in luxury manufacturing, but at Begg the effect is heightened by its location and the delicacy of the end product.

ABOVE: The cloth is carefully inspected, with some errors reweaved by hand.

RIGHT AND OPPOSITE: Begg uses a range of weaving machines, from old, slower models to the latest jacquard machinery.

A scarf specialist

The processes that go into making a scarf are similar to those involved in any type of high-end weaving. Spun yarn is required; that yarn is warped, then woven across a loom. The resulting cloth is finished with several wet and dry processes, and along the way there are constant checks and careful repairs.

It is, therefore, no coincidence that the majority of scarf manufacturers in the world also weave cloth for other purposes. The odds and ends from any weaving look like natural candidates for scarves. Among these are Loro Piana and Johnston's of Elgin – who both also offer suitings and knitwear. But not Begg. If there is one obvious way in which Begg is distinctive, it is its pure focus on scarves. 'I've seen some other factories try to add scarves to their production, but it's often more difficult than they anticipate,' says Ann Ryley, Begg's sales and marketing director. 'The finishing has to be different, of course, and there are several other steps such as fringing that can be tricky to get right.'

Many of those larger competitors do get it right, of course, but perhaps the greatest advantage to making just scarves is the focus it brings to design. When scarves are an afterthought, their design is even more so: plain colours in similar tones to the rest of the production (for simplicity and efficiency) and standard finishing. Or, worse: garish, ill-considered patterns and multicoloured stripes; the kind one might be encouraged to wear to 'cheer up' an outfit.

Begg has stood out in this way, taking time over its selection of colours and introducing subtle variation every year. But in recent times that innovation has increased, with new finishing and textural effects, and the odd colour combination that stands out because of its simplicity and sophistication.

The new Begg & Co.

Four years ago the company decided to relaunch its own label. It had always sold its own scarves under the 'Alex Begg' name, but the majority of the business was third-party work for the big couture houses. It wanted to increase its own share of production – always higher margin and more stable

ABOVE: Two of the older machines at Begg, creating the warp of the cloth and then weaving across it.

OPPOSITE: Ends are tied off, while teasels lie in racks, ready to be used to comb the cloth.

than third-party work – and take it upmarket. Under the new brand, Begg & Co., the company launched new men's and women's ranges, with Michael Drake looking after the former and Angela Bell the latter. In common with the company's general approach, both designers were selected for their specialization in accessories, rather than general fashion, and their connection to the manufacturing side of the business.

The new scarves brought in more colours, more muted and modern tones, and, importantly, expanded the range for men. 'Previously the lightweight scarves were really only designed for women, but a lot of men were buying them as well. So we purposely introduced a full range of lightweights in more masculine colours,' says Ann. It was Ann herself who was responsible for one of the most significant innovations. With the aim of creating a casual range, which would appeal to a younger market but sacrifice none of Begg's luxurious touch, Ann experimented with washing a range of finished scarves.

Any woven product goes through rounds of washing ('wet' finishing) in order to soften it. This leads to a rather bedraggled effect, which is carefully ironed out through several rounds of dry finishing. Taking that beautifully pressed product and washing it all over again puzzled many in the factory, and even angered some. But the slightly distressed result – particularly the washed Kishorn – has proved extremely popular.

'It was rather contrary to the traditions of the company, which had always been driving towards that perfect, silky finish,' says Ann. 'But its success has made people realize the need in the market for a more relaxed, informal product – one that a man might wear with a leather jacket at the weekend, while the regular Kishorn goes with his cashmere overcoat during the week.'

Among the other innovations have been new versions of classic Begg products, often derived from unique manufacturing processes. The Nuance, for example, is a scarf that fades from one colour to another along its length. It involves hand-dyeing the colour change in the yarn before weaving it together into the scarf. This is both difficult and expensive; the only alternative is to dip-dye the scarf after it is woven, which creates a much starker gradation.

Begg recently expanded the Nuance range with lightweight and washed versions, as well as offering them in those new, masculine colours: marble and grey, or indigo and navy. In fact, many of the combinations are influenced by the sea or landscape – one advantage of Begg's rugged Scottish surroundings.

Other distinctive Begg processes produce its ripple finish and its Wispy scarves. The ripple finish is achieved with the combination of an old wooden milling machine, which pummels the cloth, and brushing it with dried plant heads called teasels. While other manufacturers also use teasels, Begg believes its arrangement of the heads is unique, and the finished ripple effect certainly is. The Wispy, on the other hand, is an ultra-fine, lightweight scarf, created from five miles of cashmere. The yarn is so fine that it would snap if woven normally, so a patented process is used that combines it with a synthetic fibre called Keralon. The two are woven together and then the scarf is finished, with the Keralon dissolving in the wash.

Echoes of the past

Given this cutting-edge production, it's hard to believe that Begg is almost 150 years old. Founded in 1866 in the town of Paisley, it was at the centre of the growth in Scottish weaving at the time. Begg was even partly responsible for the paisley patterns that have now become more famous than the town itself. The two earliest remaining examples of paisley shawls were made by the company: one is kept on public display in the Paisley Museum, while the other is owned by a member of the Begg family. Begg has been based in Ayr since 1902. It's tempting to see in those years an echo of the recent spurt of innovation – for the company's move presaged a period of investment in machinery and experimentation with new techniques, just as there has been recently.

'Although the company has gone through a lot of changes over the years, it's not too much to say that this approach – this constant searching for new ways of doing things – has always been part of our DNA,' says Ann. 'It's our responsibility to keep it going now for the next 150 years.'

ABOVE AND OPPOSITE: Workers carefully check the cloth for stray ends and imperfections.

BRENT BLACK

THE FINEST PANAMA HATS IN THE WORLD

CROWNED WITH PALM LEAVES

BRENT B. BLACK – NOT A NAME YOU FORGET IN A HURRY – IS FANATICAL ABOUT RESURRECTING FINE PANAMA HAT WEAVING. HE HAS HIS OWN SCHOOL, HIS OWN CHARITY AND, MOST IMPORTANTLY, HIS OWN WEAVERS.

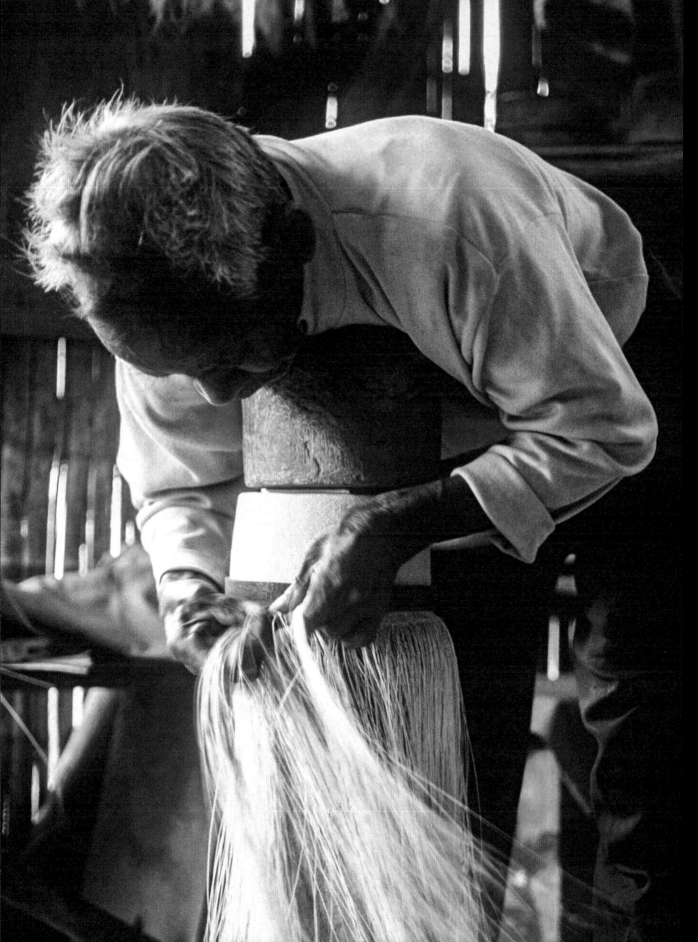

Panama hats are not from Panama. I'm sure you know that, but it's a good place to start. They're woven in Ecuador, but used to be shipped from Panama because it was more convenient, and they acquired the name of their point of export among early adopters in the US and Europe. International media coverage of the building of the Panama Canal helped increase popularity, particularly when President Roosevelt visited the site and was pictured wearing one.

Today, the Panama hat is a mass-produced menswear standard. But it is possible to find truly extraordinary hats: hats that take months for someone to weave, carefully and painstakingly, by hand. Brent Black, although an American based in Hawaii, has become the source of the finest bespoke Panamas through his personal involvement with these craftsmen.

To find the finest Panamas today you need to seek out the weavers in Montecristi, a town on the Pacific coast of Ecuador – or rather, the weavers around the town of Montecristi, as most of them work from their homes on the outskirts of town. It is the related craftsmen – the *apaleadors*, *cortadors* and *planchadors* – who work in the centre and serve several weavers, as well as the local dealers.

ABOVE AND OPPOSITE: Whether drying or stacked awaiting work, Panamas look attractive around the streets of Montecristi.

ABOVE AND RIGHT: Panama hats are part of the culture in Montecristi – the heart of the finest hat-weaving in the world.

From plant to beehive

The making of a hat begins with the farming of *cogollos*: long, green spikes that, if left to mature, will open up into a spread of palm leaves about a metre wide. The weaver wants the youngest, most undeveloped leaf shoots in the centre of the spikes. He must first pick the *cogollos* when they are at the right point of development and then peel back the tough outer layer and a few tougher shoots to reveal a long, pale-coloured fan in the middle. Even the edges of this accordion are too tough, so he uses the tip of a deer antler to slice them off, leaving a few dozen long, tender strips. Although pale, these strips (*tallos*) are still definitely green, vegetal and leaf-like. It is only after several stages of sulphur application, including two smokings and a lot of beating, that they get the creamy colour we associate with Panamas. First, though, they must be boiled: curled up into a pot and stirred over a fire. They are then hung up outside – on washing lines if the sun is not too strong, or in the shade.

Next is one of the more unhealthy stages of Panama hat-making: the *tallos* are placed in a white wooden box – similar in size and structure to a beehive – and burning sulphur is placed underneath. Hot coals keep the sulphur smoking and it rises up through the box, bleaching the straws.

ABOVE: *Tallos* are dried by hanging from the roofs – inside or outside the workers' houses.

OPPOSITE: Two early stages in the making of the *tallos*: they are farmed in the surrounding jungle and then the outer layers are cut off with the tip of a deer antler. In the bottom right image, the outer casings are being gradually discarded in favour of the more tender central shoots.

ABOVE: The *tallos* must be boiled, dried and then bleached with sulphur.

ABOVE: The weaving begins by working with just four crossed pairs of straws, creating a centre to the top of the hat.

OPPOSITE: Weaving the brim. A leather strap keeps the crown in place while the worker bends over the hat and works the brim outwards.

Weaving the straw

The weaving of a hat begins with four crossed pairs of straws, which are then interwoven and gradually expanded with the addition of more straws to create the *plantilla* – the circle that forms the top of the hat. You can always tell a weaver by his hands, because he has long, carefully maintained thumb nails, which are used to split the straws prior to weaving, creating exactly the right thickness and length. When the *plantilla* is as big as the top of a hat, it is placed on a wooden block or form, which sits on a wooden platform at about waist height. The weaver bends over and places his chest on top of the block to hold the hat in place as he continues to weave around its edges, bending the edge down over the wooden form. These extended periods of pressure on the chest are not good for weavers, but thankfully today they take regular breaks.

When the crown is large enough and it is time to start weaving the brim, a leather strap is tied tightly around the bottom of the hat. The weaver then starts weaving outwards and, when he has finished, leaves 12 to 14 centimetres of excess straw around the edge. He does not finish the brim: that is the job of a *rematadora*. This is a specialized job that involves weaving the straws back again, towards the crown. Even the final tightening is done by someone else, the *azocador*. The *cortador* then trims off the loose ends and after washing and bleaching (involving more sulphur), it is over to the *apaleador* to pound the hats with a wooden mallet to soften them.

This last job is my favourite. It is the *apaleador*'s strong-armed work that produces the characteristic colour of panamas, as he hammers them and regularly sprinkles sulphur powder on and between the hats. The contrast between the delicate weaving and the brutal force of the *apaleador* is striking. It also shows how fragile raw materials can be woven into something that is pliable and strong.

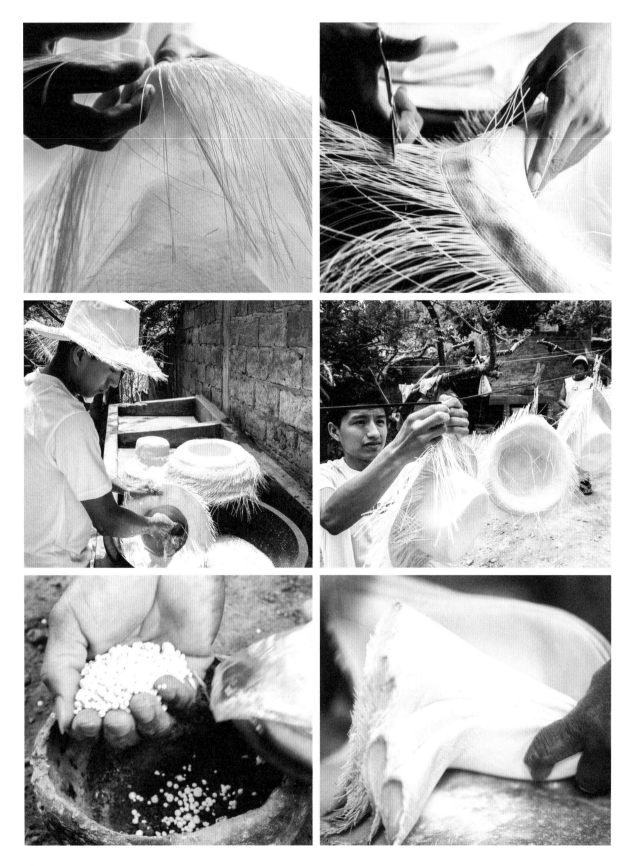

ABOVE: The *apaleador* sprinkles sulphur between hats before hammering them, which creates the distinctive bleached colour of a Panama.

OPPOSITE, FROM THE TOP: Back-weaving the brim, cutting off the excess, washing, drying, sulphur for bleaching and the sulphur being applied to the hats.

On to Brent Black

Now we know how the hats are created, we come to the role of Brent Black, of Kailua, Hawaii. Brent makes the finest bespoke Panama hats in the world, by blocking them himself and personally employing the best weavers in Montecristi. Clients largely order online, using precisely sized hat bands sent in the post. Brent then regularly travels to Ecuador to monitor the process and look after his various charitable projects.

Brent set up his company in 1988 with the mission, as he saw it, of rescuing the art of fine hat-weaving in Montecristi. For 15 years he bought hats within the existing system, under which many middlemen made more money than the weavers (even the guy driving them from the weaver's house into town) and there was no practice of rewarding finer work.

Today, Brent employs some of the finest weavers and buys directly from others. He has also set up a school to help pass on the requisite skills and some of the weavers spend their time teaching as well as working. His only competitor in this regard is the Ecuadorean government, which has lately realized the value of local skills and set up its own training programme.

THIS PAGE AND OPPOSITE:
Hat-weaving is a family affair in Montecristi, with many generations and relations involved.

Blocking a SOB

When the hats arrive in Hawaii they are a uniform shape. They have no style. For each individual order, Brent has to pick a raw hat that best suits the model, size and proportions of his customer and block it accordingly. This means that a particular quality (and therefore price) cannot be guaranteed.

Blocking involves steaming the hat to soften it – usually filling up the inside of the crown, so it relaxes evenly all round – and pulling it firmly onto an appropriate wooden block. There is a different block for each style and size. A cinch cord is then tightened around the hat to keep it in place and the hat is pulled down tightly. A wooden boomerang-shaped tool can be used to pull the hat taut and a 'tipper', the inverse of the top of the block, is pressed on top to shape the crown. Unfortunately, it's not always this simple. As Brent likes to say, hats are unpredictable little SOBs. Some stretch a lot and some stretch very little; they are made from natural straw, after all. This can be frustrating when you are trying to get measurements to within an eighth of an inch and working with precious raw material.

'Sometimes I can block four or five before the straw behaves as it's supposed to,' he says. 'The price is the same, though, no matter how many wasted efforts there are. That's the problem when you deal in such fine details.' The crown has to be pressed with 65 pounds of hot sand, to smooth it and set the shape. Last of all, a leather sweatband is inserted and the exterior hat band (both made to size) is hand-sewn on the outside with silk thread. Some manufacturers destroy good hats by using a sewing machine or thick cotton thread.

A work of art on the head

There may be more individual craft in a Panama hat than anything else included in this book – from the selection of the raw material right through to the final product, shipped to the customer in a specially designed hat box. The end result is a beautiful thing, perching crown-like atop a gentleman's head. Men might have long eschewed the felt fedora or trilby, but when the sun's out they all need a Panama. Now we just have to make sure they buy one from Brent.

ABOVE: Blocking can be a frustrating experience, with several attempts sometimes needed to get the right shape, with much re-measuring in between.

OPPOSITE: Sixty-five pounds of hot sand, covered with layers of asbestos and cotton, are lowered onto the hat to set the shape.

BRESCIANI

THE FINEST SOCKS
IN THE WORLD

A FAMILY AFFAIR

BRESCIANI HAS BEEN ONE OF ITALY'S TOP SOCK MANUFACTURERS FOR DECADES, BUT RECENTLY EXPANDED TO CREATE ITS OWN BRAND, BECOMING A BYWORD FOR QUALITY IN THE PROCESS.

ABOVE: The Bresciani facility outside Bergamo.

OPPOSITE: The factory has a large store of yarn colours, which are needed for its broad range of designs.

Massimiliano Bresciani runs the Bresciani factory in Spirona, just outside of Bergamo in northern Italy. At least he does in theory. His father, Mario, is still around the factory every day, despite being in his seventies. A floating presence – a conscience, even – Mario walks the factory floor picking up socks and turning them over, inspecting them. 'I arrive at around 7.15 in the morning, and my father is always here,' says Massimiliano. 'He goes home for a few hours in the afternoon, but he will frequently be here until the factory closes at 7 or 8 pm. His most important role today is training – helping the women who operate each of the 13 quality-control stages. That's crucial for us and is a difficult thing to teach. Even though 95% of the production is now done by electronic machines, his experience is indispensable.'

Massimiliano jokes that his mother is glad to have Mario out of the house. She can't stand having him at home all day, watching and inspecting the cooking – just as he has done for decades at the factory. It's not the kind of thing you can just turn off.

Starting a factory

Mario began working when he was 12 after his father died from injuries sustained during the Second World War. He had two younger siblings, aged ten and eight, so he went to work. He found a job in Milan, 42 kilometres away, and cycled there every day.

By the age of 15, Mario had moved into the sock business, joining Caiza Bloch. Bergamo has been a textile centre since the Second World War, when

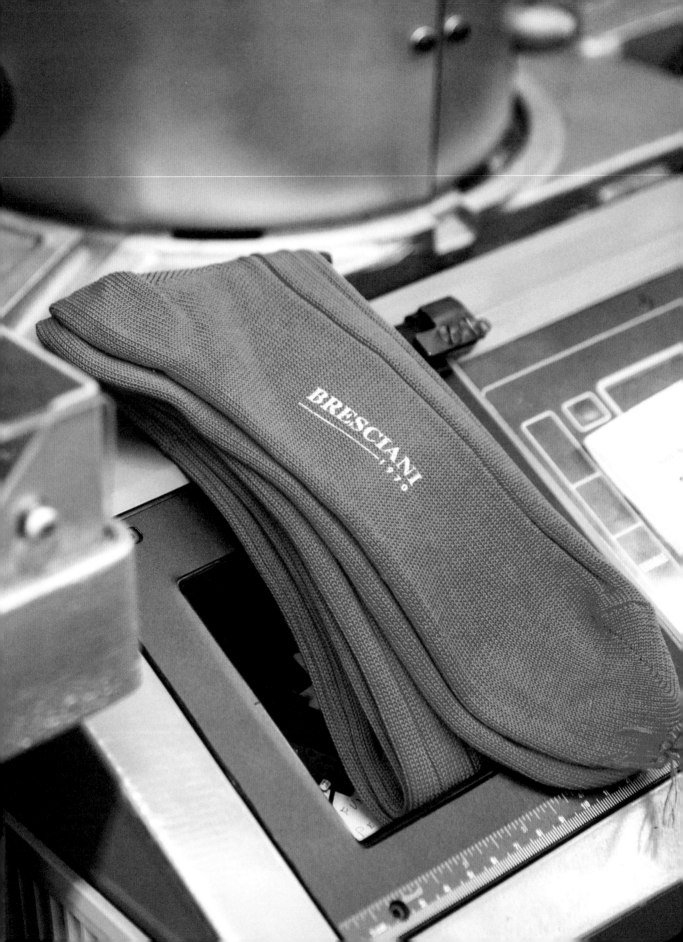

several Swiss cotton companies moved down into the valleys in the north of the region to make use of the rivers for cleaning the cloth and powering their mills. Silk spinning was another early industry in the area and that was where Massimiliano's mother was employed.

After a number of years, Mario became the head of production at Caiza Bloch. He left when the company started to falter, going first to Gallo, one of only two or three remaining Italian sock manufacturers aside from Bresciani, until, in the late sixties, he arrived home one night with a big pile of papers.

'My mother always tells the story of how he came through the door carrying this stack of the documents you had to sign in those days to get a loan. He sat down at the kitchen table and told her, more as a courtesy than anything else, that they now had their own company and they had quite a lot of debts to pay off,' says Massimiliano. Money from the loan also paid for four sock-making machines, which were initially stored in the garage.

By 1970 – the year Massimiliano was born – the business had grown enough to justify opening a dedicated factory. Sitting in Mario's office, you are surrounded by evidence of the history of his work. While employed at Caiza Bloch, he worked with knitwear company Avon (now Avon Celli) and kept the archives of this work after Caiza Bloch closed down. A few dozen pages are displayed around the walls.

ABOVE: Extracts from the Caiza Bloch archive.

OPPOSITE: A finished pair of cotton socks await inspection.

Two more Avon books greet you as you walk into the building and a couple more are displayed in the hall outside. They show row upon row of swatches, from the styles sold in the 1950s and 1960s. The colours are muted, but the patterns are extremely intricate.

Delicate machines

Bresciani's many sock-weaving machines divide into five types: for jacquards, micro-patterns, large weaves, Argyles and delicate materials such as silk and cashmere. They all work the same way: two steel discs knit the yarn into a long tube of cloth from cones serried around them. The sock grows up and up from the knitting teeth until it is long enough to be sucked up a tall plastic tube and dropped, back at waist height, into a metal basket.

The Argyle machine is the most complex. It has 25 cones of yarn haloed above it, all feeding different colours into a series of small mechanical arms that tap out the pattern. No wonder good Argyle socks are so hard to find.

ABOVE AND BELOW: The Argyle knitting machine is the most complex, with the greatest number of cones having to feed in from the top.

OPPOSITE: Two steel discs knit the socks together, gradually creating a tube that emerges below.

ABOVE: Heated sock shapes are used to press the finished garment, some of which have a rather smiley demeanour when the toe seam is upturned.

OPPOSITE: The tube of knitted cotton emerges from the bottom of a knitting machine.

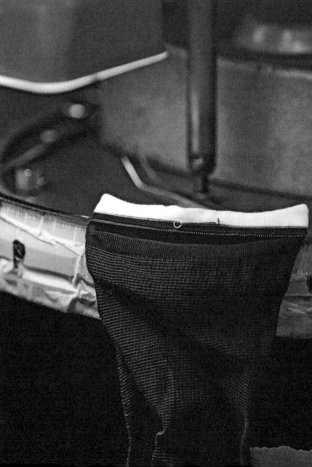

All that is required now is to sew the tube together across the top of the toe. A group of women sit along one wall, placing both sides of the sock onto a large-toothed wheel so it can be stitched together. The skill is to sit each tooth of the wheel perfectly between each thread of the sock. Each material has its own machine – silk is particularly difficult, with 260 closely packed teeth around its wheel.

Hand linking, as this process is called, used to be the sign of a good pair of socks. It is still proudly stamped by many companies on their product labels. But since 2002, when a new contraption was invented that does the same process by machine, hand linking has not been necessary. As these women retire, therefore, they are gradually being replaced by machines.

All in the family

Part of the reason Bresciani hasn't replaced all the hand-linkers is that these machines are expensive – it can only afford to buy one or two a year. But it is

ABOVE AND LEFT: The finishing process involves pressing each sock and hand-sewing each pair together.

OPPOSITE: Linking the toe is still largely done by hand, although machines are gradually taking over the process.

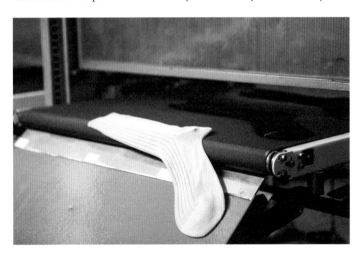

ABOVE: Sample books of new patterns and colours are created.

OPPOSITE: Occasionally, hand-sewing is still required for some tasks.

also keen to keep on staff whenever possible. Between 2005 and 2008, the company grew by 75% – partly as a result of emphasizing and marketing its own label – but it did not expand its workforce of 30. The women were more than willing to work longer hours and work different shifts in order to make production. In 2009 the company experienced its worst year ever, with revenue falling 37%, but no one was laid off. It has since recovered, with double-digit growth in 2010 and 2011.

'We feel this is a family, not just in word but in deed. We make sure the women always know about the success of the company and where it is being featured, and we have organized trips for everyone to Pitti Uomo and to Venice. This is important both for our ethics and our business – it is not easy to find people who want to work with their hands and will put passion into it,' says Massimiliano. This idea of family is literally true for about 30% of the staff. Massimiliano's wife, brother, mother, father, eldest son and two sisters-in-law all work at the company. His brother looks after production, while Massimiliano does all the travelling, sales and marketing. One sister-in-law attaches the labels to Bresciani socks and the other makes up the sample books to send to clients. Every sample book involves cutting a sock tube into strips and gluing them in by hand, before writing on the number of the style. Last year she made 9,000 of them.

Consistent innovation

Bresciani's range is one aspect that sets it apart from other sock companies. Despite being one-sixth the size of Gallo, and despite the Chinese and Korean producers that now dominate the market, Bresciani produces over 200 new designs every year, each with half-sizes in a rainbow of colours.

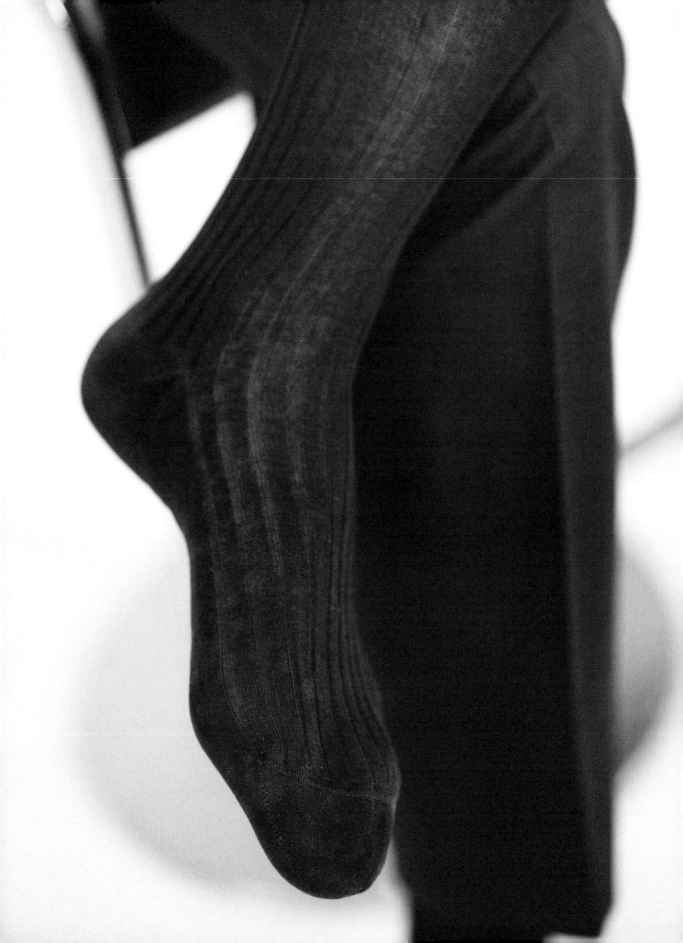

'As you would expect, about 80% of the business comes from 20% of the designs, but you need to innovate in order to stay ahead and keep customers interested,' says Massimiliano.

One of my favourite innovations is a thick cashmere sock that is stitched onto a leather sole, creating a luxurious slipper. Apparently Mario came up with the idea when he came downstairs, sleepless, after a particularly heavy dinner. His swollen feet meant rigid slippers were uncomfortable, so he swore he'd come up with an alternative.

Bresciani keeps a small archive, which contains the designs of the past five years, in one room on the top floor. They include one featuring lyrics from the national anthem, another with Shakespeare's famous 'to be or not to be' speech from *Hamlet* knitted into it and a 'dinosaur' sock that has triangles jutting out all the way up the leg. Mario's archive down the hall contains some older but treasured pieces, including a hand-drawn sketch which was a thank-you note from Jean-Louis Dumas at Hermès. Framed on the wall is also a picture of Walter Matthau, whom Mario apparently walked up to brazenly in a Hollywood restaurant as the former was having dinner with Gene Wilder. 'I am Italian maker of socks,' he said, in his broken English. He then secured Matthau's address and dropped round samples the next day.

It is no accident that such a history, with all its concomitant anecdotes and myths, is common to all the artisans in this book. But there are many others, not mentioned, that have failed to turn similar longevity into an enduring tradition. They have abandoned their mode of production under various pressures, and lost their skills and values.

Bresciani has flourished by retaining its values. Its peerless quality control, consistent innovation and open attitude to technology have made it one of the best producers of socks in the world. As a result, despite all the electronics, Mario can recognize the company as the one he founded over 40 years ago.

ABOVE: Walter Matthau, socks awaiting distribution and a thank-you note from Jean-Louis Dumas.

OPPOSITE: A finished pair of cotton, calf-length Bresciani socks.

CIFONELLI

THE FINEST SUITS
IN THE WORLD

PARISIAN HEROES

CIFONELLI TAILORING IS CHARACTERIZED
BY INTRICATE HANDWORK AND AN
EXACTING FIT. IT IS THE HOUSE'S
RESTLESS CREATIVITY, HOWEVER,
THAT SETS IT APART.

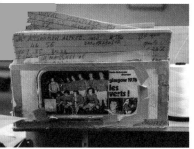

ABOVE: Cifonelli has a reputation for whimsical but beautifully made additions to traditional tailoring. Above, a sports badge created for a corduroy jacket. Below, clients' records are stored in an old cardboard box.

OPPOSITE: A lightweight navy worsted suit belonging to the author. The buttons are unique to Cifonelli, cut in a deep, matte horn.

Tailoring is the only category in this book to have two companies included: Savile Row legend Anderson & Sheppard and Parisian house Cifonelli. Bespoke tailoring is a very special trade and one dear to my heart. It is in fact two distinct crafts: cutting, the artistry of fitting two-dimensional shapes perfectly on a three-dimensional form, and tailoring, the sewing involved in padding, assembling and finishing a work of art in cloth. Two tailors have been included in this book because men want something very different from a sports jacket compared to a business suit. They are worn on different occasions and the intention is to make a very particular impression. Anderson & Sheppard makes a beautiful jacket and, as already discussed, there are particular reasons for its distinctive comfort.

But Cifonelli makes the kind of suits you dream about. Elegant yet professional, sharp but discreet. The suit for the job interview, for the first date, for making exactly the right impression. With roped shoulders, Milanese buttonholes and sweeping lapels, it is a very distinct aesthetic.

The origins of Cifonelli

It is no coincidence that the best Parisian tailors have Italian roots. Camps de Luca, Smalto and Cifonelli all combine Italian flair with very modern French chic. Cifonelli hails from Rome, founded there in 1880, and opened a shop in Paris in 1926. The French branch found an immediate following, surviving the Second World War, and grew in size through the middle of the century. The Rome atelier, on the other hand, suffered particularly from the growth of ready-to-wear fashions in Italy. By 1990 only one cutter was left. When he retired, Cifonelli became a French firm, headed by Arturo Cifonelli.

Arturo was demanding, uncompromising and passionate. He was loved and feared by his workers who, legend has it, made the sign of the cross before sending him a suit for final inspection. When Arturo died in 1972, his son

Adriano took over and carried on developing his father's work. Cifonelli slowly started to gain a reputation outside the small, stylish circle of its clientele, which included Paul Meurisse, Lino Ventura, Marcello Mastroianni and, most importantly, François Mitterrand (whose Cifonelli collection was auctioned at Drouot). In 2003, cousins Lorenzo and Massimo Cifonelli took over the running of the tailoring house from Adriano and it has gone from strength to strength, becoming the largest tailoring house in Paris. Of particular importance was the acquisition of the workshop of Gabriel Gonzalez in 2008, building on the earlier takeover of Claude Rousseau's team in 2000. Together, those acquisitions reunited the dream team that had worked at Camps de Luca over 30 years earlier.

Since taking the helm, Lorenzo, in particular, has restlessly improved the quality of the work at Cifonelli and added his own innovations in the rich tradition of French tailors such as Joseph Camps and Francesco Smalto. Lorenzo credits Claude Rousseau, in particular, for teaching him the extreme art of detail. Lorenzo frequently conducts first fittings with spare lengths of cloth, in order to gain an extra, risk-free fitting. This is particularly useful on trousers, which can be harder to alter than jackets, and on suits for female customers. He was also responsible for introducing a system whereby each basted suit is double checked before it goes for the first fitting. All the cut parts are measured and then checked against the measurements first taken from the customer to ensure no time is wasted. The basted fittings of other top-end tailors can seem like sacks in comparison.

'This is about attention to detail, sure. But, more importantly than that, it saves us time and effort. By having strict quality control among the tailors it means more things are produced at a higher standard and in a faster time. Everyone is happier,' says Lorenzo.

ABOVE: A tailor hand-stitches the waistband buttonhole on a pair of trousers. Cifonelli is known for the extent and fineness of its hand-sewing.

OPPOSITE: Lorenzo Cifonelli checks a customer's paper pattern on his cutting board.

ABOVE: Cifonelli always uses silk linings on its jackets, with the edges top-stitched for a decorative touch.

BELOW: Cousins Lorenzo and Massimo Cifonelli at their Parisian atelier.

OPPOSITE: A heavy herringbone double-breasted jacket, with bellows pockets.

Constant innovation

Lorenzo's greatest innovations, however, have been in design. The last time I was in Paris he had four new models displayed on mannequins, each with its own little novelties. The double-breasted jacket had lapels that had been cut separately and sewn onto the foreparts of the suit. This was to allow the angle of cloth in the lapel to be changed so it was on the bias – with the cut at 45 degrees to the weave – enabling more curve in the lapel. As men's tastes tend towards an open jacket that displays plenty of shirt and tie, this is a clever way of achieving a contemporary look without lowering the buttoning point to an unflattering degree.

One of the other jackets was a charcoal tweed with expansive lapels and neat patch pockets featuring diagonal buttonholes. And there was a purple velvet number with an intricate fastening mechanism. The best of the lot, though, was a green jacket in yak wool. Woven by hand and to order in Tibet, Lorenzo found a tiny supplier of the wonderfully spongy cloth a few years ago and made a jacket from it out of curiosity. He now offers it in 30 colours.

How suits are made

These unusual jackets remain outliers, and the vast majority of Cifonelli commissions are for plain, though very finely worked, business suits. Subtle differences set them apart.

In the chapter on Anderson & Sheppard, we looked at how a bespoke suit is made, with the layers of canvas in the chest and wadding in the shoulders being loosely sewn together and built into a pliable structure. Cifonelli uses loose stitches in the chest and a soft shoulder pad like Anderson & Sheppard, but there the similarities end.

Cifonelli cuts the cloth close to the chest, creating a clean finish that is very different from the Anderson & Sheppard drape. It keeps the jacket close at the waist and hips as well, leading to a simple, straight silhouette. The overall effect of these features would be of a neat but undramatic jacket, but the drama is in the shoulders. By adding a hand-constructed wad of foam at the top of the sleeve, the tailors create significant 'roping' – so-called because it looks like a thin rope is running around the inside of the sleeve, lifting it up.

Many tailors use roping in the sleeve. Cifonelli uses a slightly exaggerated form of the technique that creates a big, heroic effect with actually rather soft tailoring. There are no large, padded shoulders or rigid chests; instead the impression of breadth is achieved by giving the viewer two focal points at either end of the shoulder. If overdone, it could look rather feminine, but Cifonelli always seems to get the balance just right.

ABOVE: A tailor examines a jacket, while below, suit sections await the next stage in their construction.

OPPOSITE: The most distinctive aspect of a Cifonelli suit is its roped shoulder, which gives an impression of breadth without heavy padding.

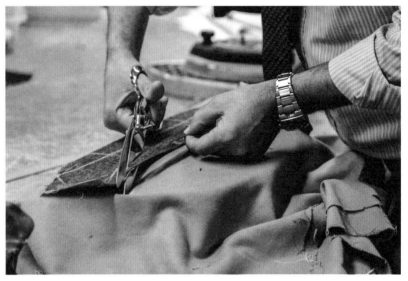

ABOVE AND OPPOSITE: A tailor chalks – and then cuts – a refinement to a flannel suit in the making. Cifonelli uses relatively lightweight pieces of canvas and horsehair in the chests of its suits. The layers are loosely sewn.

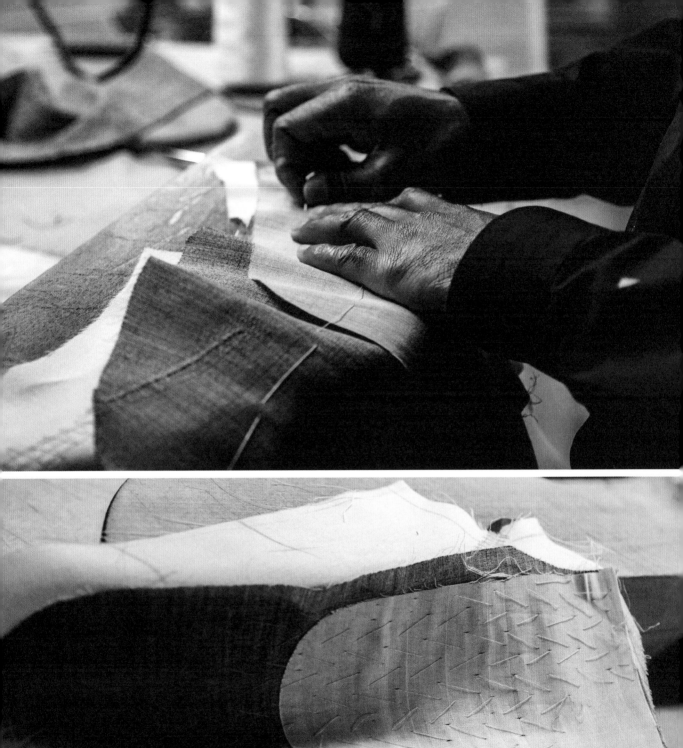

The Milanese buttonhole

Another way in which Cifonelli's garments differ is in their buttonholes. A small detail, but as the only piece of handwork that shows prominently on the outside of a suit, they are significant. The lapel buttonhole is particularly so, as it sits so high on the jacket and is never used – except, perhaps, to hold a flower on special occasions. Cifonelli, in common with most Parisian tailors, works this buttonhole particularly finely to create what is known as a Milanese finish. Although often associated with the couture tradition in Paris, the buttonhole technique originated in central Italy. (Not in Milan, as the name suggests. The name appears to have come from a type of thread involved in the process.) Today, however, it is almost unknown in Italy.

To create the fine, raised buttonhole, silk thread has to be wound tightly and carefully around a thicker length of thread known as the gimp. A normal buttonhole involves a series of tiny knots tied around that gimp. Being knots, they are necessarily thicker and the overall effect is less sleek. Winding thread may sound easier than tying knots, but the amount of precision required with the Milanese buttonhole is extraordinary. Each time the thread must be wound around, anchored through the cloth and then wound again, with precisely the same tension. If that tension varies at all, the line of the buttonhole will kink. A tailor can take up to an hour to work a perfect Milanese, concentrating on the strain he places on the thread the entire time.

Cifonelli generally uses a Milanese finish only on the lapel buttonholes. The others are worked in the traditional, knotted manner, but they are still finer than most of those made in England or Italy. While a knot can never be quite as fine, or raised, as the Milanese loop, there is still a lot of skill in stitching close to the gimp in a regular buttonhole. It is harder and it takes longer, but the effect is always noticeable.

There are dozens of other details in a Cifonelli suit that could be examined in such detail, from the handmade shoulder wadding to the traditional trouser fastening, the vintage silk linings to the signature hand-sewn 'C' on the central lining seam. But the Milanese is the crowning glory.

ABOVE: A Milanese buttonhole on the lapel of a jacket.

OPPOSITE: Fine, slanted buttonholes on the cuff of a jacket, with suede binding.

GJ CLEVERLEY & CO.

THE FINEST SHOES
IN THE WORLD

DELICATE LITTLE SCULPTURES

GJ CLEVERLEY IS ONE OF THE DRESSIEST OF ENGLISH SHOEMAKERS, SPECIALIZING IN SLIM, ELEGANT FOOTWEAR MADE TO THE HIGHEST BESPOKE STANDARDS.

Bespoke shoes begin with an act of sculpture. The last-maker takes a hammer, a chisel and a block of beech wood and slowly begins the process of carving an idealized shoe. After the chisel comes the lathe, and then finally the sandpaper, until a perfect and perfectly smooth sculpture, called a last, is created that the last-maker's fellow artisans can stretch leather around. I remember trying sculpture: it's very hard to know when to stop. A little like watercolour or, better, drawing with white chalk on black paper, the skill is working with the negative space.

The memory came back to me last year as I watched Teemu Leppänen calmly chisel a wooden last into shape. This was upstairs at GJ Cleverley's atelier in The Royal Arcade, London. The proprietor, George Glasgow, says people never believe him when he says the shoes are made upstairs. It seems a ludicrous thing to do in the middle of Mayfair – all that sawdust and elbow grease. But once you climb the spiral stairs and watch Teemu, John Carnera or any other of the Cleverley staff work, it seems the most natural thing in the world. Why wouldn't you make your product above the shop, if you could?

Of course, many of the world's tailors do the same. And, like they do, some of the work is inevitably done off-site, even if it's just round the corner in Soho. With both tailoring and shoemaking, the making of the suit or shoe is the part that is stationed outside. Cutting and last-making are too crucial to the individual customer to be that far away.

How a perfect shape is made

But let's start at the beginning. First a customer's feet are traced in the measuring book. It seems almost sacrilegious to stand on such a book, pressing your dirty soles into the pages, but then shoemaking is a dirtier business than most.

Once the basic outline has been drawn, measurements are taken around the girth of the foot to fill in the third dimension. The arch and ankle are key: these are two places where a bespoke shoe will feel markedly different from any other shoe. It will grip the foot, making the overall fit more comfortable and preventing you from slipping around inside.

ABOVE AND BELOW: The last is checked against the outline of a customer's foot.

OPPOSITE: Teemu Leppänen files down the last, checking the measurements as he goes and creating a distinctive Cleverley toe shape.

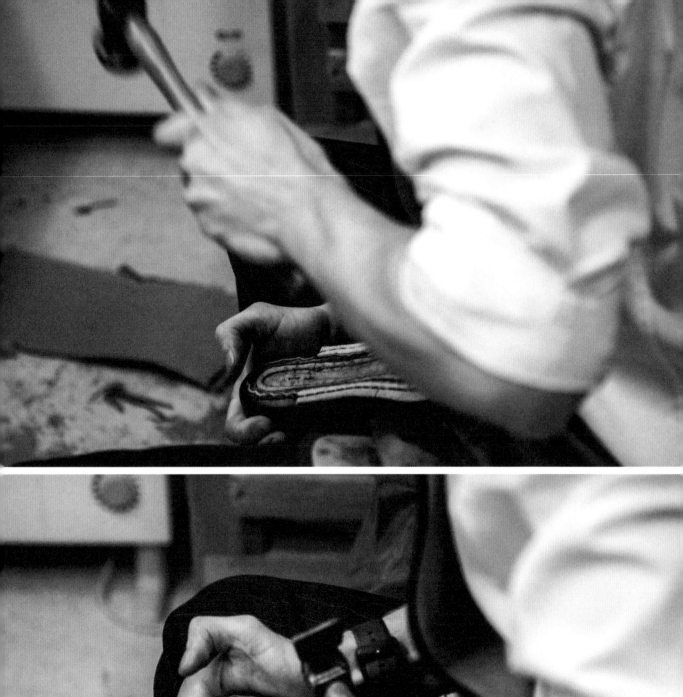

After measurements comes discussion of the order: style, leather, toe shape. There are a surprising number of choices. Then, while Teemu chips away with his chisel, someone stretches out a hide of Freudenberg leather, carefully checking it for imperfections. Cardboard shapes, representing the different pieces of the shoe on the leather, are carefully laid out and then cut out. This clicking – so named for the sound the knife makes with each incision – is key to a good pair of shoes. It enables close attention to be paid to the shapes of the pieces and the hide they come from. Some ready-to-wear shoemakers click by hand as well, but many use standard-size presses to stamp them out.

Next the pieces are closed (stitched together, off-site) before being brought back to Cleverley HQ to be checked and stretched over the last. The reason this stage is done in-house is that the person checking will also have taken the initial measurements, so he can ensure the shoe at this stage fits his image of the customer's foot. He will later conduct the fitting as well.

The stretching on of the leather – which is known as 'lasting' – is not for the weak-hearted. It requires a tremendous amount of force with a pair of heavy iron pliers. A white line is drawn down the centre of the toe as a guide, so the craftsman can make sure the shoe remains centralized as he forces it this way and that. He stretches the upper over the toe first, securing it with a nail that is hammered in with those same pliers. That's one benefit of their weight: it saves switching to a hammer.

ABOVE AND BELOW: Shoes sit around the workshop above The Royal Arcade, London, in various stages of make. Some have their welts attached to the upper of the shoe; the next stage is to attach them to the sole.

OPPOSITE: A shoe under work, with the welt (the pale leather strip) hand-stitched around the outside.

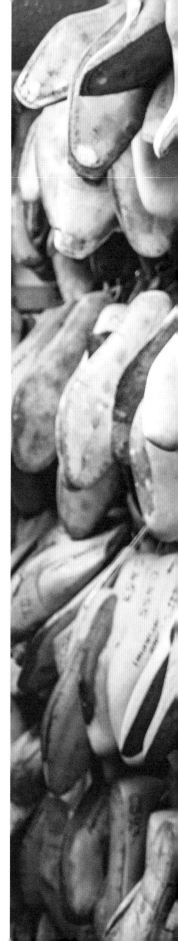

Two nails are put in either side of the toe, to maintain the centralization before the rest of the shoe is slowly filled in. The ideal tension on the leather is quite easy to gauge: it stretches so far and then no further. At that point there is no looseness or slack anywhere on the shoe: it is drum-tight. Lasting is an art, rather like making the last itself. By contrast, the final stage of stitching the welt and the sole requires concentration and strength, but is fairly standardized.

Protecting a tradition

When English shoes are described as handmade today, it usually means they are placed by hand into an old iron machine that is a substitute for a man's strength. Different machines are used for lasting, stitching and adding the sole. This is how shoes are made by the great firms of Northampton: John Lobb, Edward Green, Church's. But these shoes are not really handmade – a better term is 'benchmade', which harks back to the Industrial Revolution, when shoes moved from a cordwainer's lap to the bench of an iron machine. Benchmade shoes are a long way from modern digital manufacturing, but they are equally distant from bespoke shoemaking such as that practised at Cleverley.

The first recorded use of a last in shoemaking comes from Greek antiquity. Plato referred in his *Symposium* to how Zeus, when he created man, smoothed out the wrinkles on his torso with 'the tool with which the shoemaker smooths out creases in leather'. Although this tradition was passed down through generations, it almost died out in the Middle Ages when poverty necessitated the mere stitching together of pieces of leather in an approximate shape. The last was rediscovered in the 16th century, providing a lot of documentary evidence on contemporary designs and techniques. By the middle of the 18th century, we have full-page illustrations from technical manuals showing all the tools a bespoke shoemaker uses today – from an awl to pliers.

The Cleverley story

George Cleverley was born in 1898 into a shoemaking family. When he was two years old he moved to Colchester in Essex, where he spent his childhood selling bootlaces and polish. He followed the family profession and apprenticed as a shoemaker, but joined the army as soon as he finished the apprenticeship at age 15. He was stationed in London and then moved to a boot-making factory in Calais. After the First World War, he joined Tuczec, a grand old name in shoemaking which was at that time stationed in Clifford Street, just around the corner from the current Cleverley premises. George remained at Tuczec for 38 years, leaving in 1958 to start his own business. It was there that he perfected the chisel-shaped toe that has become synonymous with Cleverley.

Unfortunately, he fell out with his brother Anthony, who had also been at Tuczec, and Anthony set up shop at home with a few private clients. The two never spoke again, but Anthony's more aggressive last shape has recently been brought back into the Cleverley fold – along with his records of bespoke designs. Clients can now experience two different takes on the Cleverley aesthetic.

George died in 1991 at the age of 93, working to the end. He handed over to George Glasgow, who had worked with him for 20 years. Recently, management was passed to George's son, George Jr. As many craft-based companies around the world have discovered, keeping things in the family is a great way to preserve tradition. This doesn't mean tradition should be maintained for its own sake: it has to continue to be practical and valuable. The time-honoured methods of bespoke shoemaking – sculpting a last specific to a man's foot – continue to create a superior fit. You may not realize it fully for several weeks of wear, but that perfect hold on the ankle will ensure permanent comfort.

Then there are the aesthetic benefits, which capture the attention long after a bespoke customer has got used to perfect fit. A pitched and curved heel gives a shape to a shoe that a machine cannot replicate. The waist under the sole is cut close and subtly rounded, giving an appearance of lightness to the shoe that is instantly recognizable on fellow pedestrians. It is, indeed, as if someone had sculpted a perfect shoe – the finest shoe in the world – around the wearer's feet.

ABOVE: The Cleverley workshop is decorated with tools and shoe trees.

OPPOSITE: The Cleverley badge nailed to a shoe tree.

DRAKE'S

THE FINEST TIES
IN THE WORLD

THE ART OF UNDERSTATEMENT
DRAKE'S TIES BRING TOGETHER
THE BEST OF ENGLISH AND ITALIAN
AESTHETICS, CREATING SUBTLE,
SOPHISTICATED NECKWEAR.

A decadent fountain of silk, an establishment stripe, a loose counter-cultural knit: the tie is a varied symbol. To some, no suit is complete without one. Certainly, it is the natural focus of an outfit. It anchors the eye, before leading one upwards towards the face. It can be a powerful, elegant, magnificent object.

Making a tie is actually quite a simple process. First you need a square of silk. Originally, this would have been folded in on itself seven to nine times (depending on the desired width of tie) and then stitched along the back. But manufacturers quickly realized that a lining of cotton or wool produced the

OPPOSITE: Tie sections are marked on the silk and cut out in turn. Particular care has to be taken to match patterns.

BELOW: An untipped tie from Drake's. The rest of the tie will still be lined, to retain sufficient body to knot well.

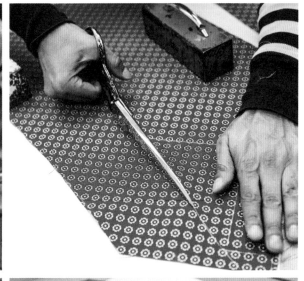

same effect and it meant that you got two ties out of the same piece of silk. So, today, the vast majority of ties have a lining and the silk contains just three folds. Some tie makers still make five, seven, or nine folds, but they usually use a lining anyway and the result is only superior in terms of its technical skill.

How a tie is made

Cardboard shapes for the various pieces of the tie – front blade, back blade, neck, keeper and tipping – are laid upon a square of silk and then cut around with a knife. Some makers will cut one piece of silk at a time, others 15 or 20. As long as it is done by hand and takes into account the nature of the silk when deciding how high to pile it, then it doesn't make much difference.

The front blade, neck and back blade are then sewn together (by sewing machine – no advantage to handwork here) and the tipping is attached to each end. Then the lining is laid in one long strip, before the tie can be sewn up. Next is the only really important bit: the slip stitch. The tie-maker (usually a woman, while the cutter is usually a man; the stereotype is the same in ties as in tailoring, in Italy as in England) tacks the two sides of the thick end of the tie together, weighs them down with a convenient lump of metal and proceeds to sew up the rest in large, looping movements. At the far end, the tie-maker leaves an inch or two of excess thread before knotting off.

This excess, along with the looseness of the stitch, allows the sides of the tie to move. It breathes life into it. When you hang the tie up at the end of the day this stitch enables it to relax back into its normal shape. During the day, it prevents it from squaring up and lets it hang naturally. It's beautifully simple: one stitch and the tie is born. After that, most things about a tie are a matter of design and taste. And there, Drake's is one of the best.

ABOVE: Silk pieces tied together before the next stage in production begins.

OPPOSITE: Bulk orders are cut with several layers of silk together, though still by hand.

ABOVE: The weight of the lining varies between styles, but is usually proportionate to the weight and weave of the silk.

OPPOSITE: Hand-stitching is used on the back of the tie – here, to attach the keeper. Crucially, it is also used to sew the slip stitch, which attaches the two sides of the tie and allows it to move along its length.

The history of Drake's

Drake's was founded in 1977 by three ex-Aquascutum employees, including Michael Drake (menswear design) and Jeremy Hull (export sales). 'It always helps when you found a business to have people who don't step on each other's toes,' says Michael. 'Looking back on it, if our areas had overlapped then it probably wouldn't have lasted.'

Jeremy left Aquascutum first, working with the department store El Corte Inglés in Spain before moving to the Italian brand Belvest. The latter wanted Jeremy to take on the brand in all English-speaking countries and he, in turn, recruited Michael. Michael was soon travelling to the US to sell Belvest to the Americans, designing his own US-specific samples each time.

'That was great experience, because it was both sales and designing a mini collection, making sure all the construction details were just as we wanted them,' remembers Michael. But although it was frantic during the selling season, it wasn't a year-round job, so in his spare time he began designing scarves.

Michael had ample experience in design, having done the house check at Aquascutum and started a small accessories collection there. He had always wanted to expand into scarves, but hadn't had the chance. He now used his time off to design a small collection of lambswool scarves, oversized and in bright colours. On a whim, he and Jeremy decided to take them to the SEHM trade show in Paris, hiring the smallest booth in the place. They took £100,000 of orders, but lost them in the airport on the way back.

Jeremy, it turned out, had picked up somebody else's briefcase. Fortunately, they managed to recover the right one and the orders in it. The pair took on premises at 25 Old Bond Street – where Tiffany & Co. is now – and developed the collection, with the Belvest business largely responsible for funding their personal project.

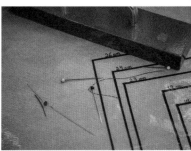

ABOVE: The trappings of a tie-maker's board: a pin cushion made from tie silk; a rubber thimble; a weight; and marks indicating different lengths of tie.

OPPOSITE: A finished Drake's tie proudly displays the fact that it has been made in England, at the east London factory.

From scarves to ties

In the mid-1980s, as Michael travelled with his scarves and with Belvest,
more and more customers began asking him where he bought his ties.
He had always been particular about ties, having them made at Holliday &
Brown or Charles Hill. He would commission them and often do interesting
things with the cloth such as inverting the colours (as he had done in tartan on
that first collection of scarves) or having them made inside out.

A customer of Michael's in Munich urged him to start making them. Not
wanting to compete with his friend Charles Hill, Michael offered to launch
it together – as Hill & Drake. It took off immediately, proving popular with
existing scarf customers. Turnbull & Asser, however, a big customer of
Charles's, was keen to secure its own supply and bought the Charles Hill
premises soon after. (It still owns and runs them today.) Michael and Jeremy
were left with customers, but no production, so they started travelling
around the country, hiring tie-makers. They moved them into their office in
Clerkenwell, London, and the Drake's tie label entered its penultimate phase.
I say penultimate because although Drake's went on to be an incredibly
successful tie business, supplying the couture houses as well as the best
menswear shops around Europe (and receiving the Queen's Award for
Export Achievement), it wasn't until it launched its website in 2007 that
the company we know today became fully fledged.

The Belvest agency work had been handed back by this time, so everyone
could focus on Drake's. Keen to expand, they began to negotiate for premises
on Savile Row. Frustratingly, the negotiations fell through, but it spurred
Michael and everyone else to launch a website.

It was modern, it was clean, it worked (always important on the internet),
and it sold to everyone, everywhere. Michael had always said that the key to
success was being able to sell to both the fashionable and the traditional, the
French, the Italians and the Americans. The site did that and it enabled the
company to spread that design sensibility around the world.

A shop finally opened in 2011 on Clifford Street, round the corner from
Savile Row. Just as the website had pushed Michael to expand into knitwear,
shirts and gloves, the shop gave the impetus for beautiful, unlined jackets,
desert boots and brogues. The Drake's aesthetic – English as worn by the
French – could all be bought in one place.

Finally, the look of the thing

Michael recently retired and was replaced by his long-time protégé Michael Hill. The aesthetic has been faithfully maintained, so it is to the younger Michael that we turn for an explanation of the dyes and materials that go into a Drake's tie. 'We don't do much ink-jet printing, which is how most mass production ties have their silk printed. Instead we use dye-and-discharge hand-screen printing, where each colour layer is printed separately onto the silk, penetrating it each time,' he explains.

To do this, two people must stand either side of a sheet of silk with a frame and then press the dye on, taking care to apply pressure evenly all the way across. The two of them often have to be similar in height to ensure consistent pressure. With ink-jet printing, by contrast, the colours are machine printed in one go on top of a generally white base cloth, and that base colour is just omitted in the printed pattern.

'Our method takes longer, is more expensive and more labour intensive,' says Michael. 'But we think it produces a richer hand. Ink-jet has its merits and can be useful in certain situations, such as lighter summer colours, but anything deeper – particularly ancient madder – needs that lustre in the cloth.'

Then there are the designs. 'A lot of the basics are inherited,' says Michael, referring to the body of work that Michael Drake and his colleagues have built up over the past 30 years. 'Our design philosophy is very much about strong British traditions, about a soft, slightly aged look. It is traditional English style, but softened to make it more versatile and international in appeal,' he explains.

'We are also always careful to think of any tie not in isolation, but with the jacket or shirt it will go with. From strongly striped shirts to bright tweeds and simple business suits, each design has this in mind.'

It is an aesthetic that necessarily speaks in abstracts, in ideas rather than rules. But it is startlingly consistent and internationally appealing. Pair that with the essential, but simple, hand-stitching of a tie, which Drake's still does entirely at its London factory, and the result is the best in the world.

ABOVE: Spotted ties with keepers inserted, waiting the hand tacks that will secure them against the tie.

OPPOSITE: A great benefit of having design and production in the same London location is the access and reference to silks from past and present collections.

ALFRED DUNHILL

THE FINEST BAGS
IN THE WORLD

HIDE, NEEDLE AND WAX
HAND-SEWING A BAG, LIKE A PAIR
OF SHOES, GIVES IT UNPARALLELED
STRENGTH AND ENDURANCE.
DUNHILL IS ONE OF THE FEW
BRANDS STILL PURSUING
THIS CRAFT.

ABOVE: Leather panels are prepared and straps fixed.

OPPOSITE: Only the finest workers, often with decades of experience in the industry, work at the Dunhill facilities in London.

Nothing ages like a good leather bag. Its large panels provide a broad canvas for the weather, physical wear and tear, and natural oils to paint a variegated patina. Leather shoes and accessories can produce the same effect in miniature, but they can't compare to the scale of beautifully weathered luggage. To look better (and more personal) year after year, the bag must be made of the finest vegetable-tanned leather and be oiled regularly to prevent the skin from drying out. Indeed, the pattern of strokes and swirls with which the owner polishes is one of the factors that make the patina unique.

But this is not a chapter about the rewards – emotional, even spiritual – of taking the time to polish and maintain leather. It is about the maker of the finest handmade bags in the world.

It's a small world

Very few traditional luggage-makers still exist in the UK. The craft is no different from dozens of others in that way. What is unusual, however, is that London is its centre. The big houses – Asprey, Dunhill, Tanner Krolle – have fluctuated in size over the years and master craftsmen have flowed from one to the other. The workshop featured here – Dunhill's operation in Walthamstow, north-east London – actually used to belong to Tanner Krolle, and several of the staff moved over to Dunhill.

Rick Read was one of those who moved. He has been practising the same craft since 1977 and is now one of two workers in Walthamstow entrusted with Dunhill's bespoke service and the making of prototypes for the London Tradition line – the brand name given to the handmade luggage produced by

this workshop. (Other 'Dunhill' bags are made in Italy. While still fine pieces, they are not hand-sewn.) Rick, however, is on the verge of retirement, so a new apprentice is being hired. Dunhill's global size is a considerable asset here: it can afford to invest in people and training where others don't have the volume of orders to do so. If the UK had more groups like this, along the lines of Chanel or Hermès in France, who see it as their responsibility to preserve similar crafts, British industry would be in better shape.

The other bespoke craftsman in Walthamstow is Tomasz Nosarzewski. While not verging on retirement like Rick, Tomasz still has decades of experience. When we met at the factory, his experience and enthusiasm were evident in the brightness of his eyes as he answered questions about technique. Not many people ask him about the time it takes to hand-ink the cut edges of a bag.

A few years ago, Dunhill relaunched its bespoke service at Bourdon House in London, following increased customer interest in both quality and personalization. It started when Tomasz visited Dunhill stores in Asia, following the opening of the brand's 'home' in Shanghai. For the first time, they were offering not just a made-to-order service, where existing models could be made in more unusual leathers, but a creative exercise that began with abstract discussion and pencil sketches. Usually these involved a specific requirement – a box to carry and display perfume samples, perhaps – and progressed to rough designs before a sample was made from *salpa*. This cheap, cardboard-like material has much of the structure and rigidity of leather, but can be cut and remodelled, bits torn off and added on. It is a glimpse into the design process any new Dunhill bag goes through, with prototypes being worked and repeatedly improved.

ABOVE AND OPPOSITE: Leather panels are carefully cut by hand, paying attention to the nature of the skin, its colouration and stretch.

The Walthamstow factory

But I digress. Let's return to Walthamstow and the craftsmanship that goes into London Tradition bags. The process of bagmaking is similar the world over (though the French do have a penchant for treated board and nails, rather than leather and thread). It also has a good deal in common with shoemaking.

Bags are made in small quantities, perhaps three to five at a time. Every part is carefully hand-cut and bundled together for the maker, who will complete one bag from start to finish. Two skills are central to this process: stitching and inking. The first is a technique common to leatherwork and key to other areas such as saddlery and shoemaking. It is the method by which the welt and sole are stitched on bespoke shoes, for example, like those from GJ Cleverley already described. The method is very strong and – importantly – cannot be replicated by a machine. It is called many things, but is most commonly referred to as the saddle stitch.

The technique involves two needles, each containing hand-waxed linen thread, being pushed through a hole in the leather from different directions. They are pulled tight, looped round, and passed again through the following hole. This interlooping makes the stitch particularly robust, but cannot be performed by a machine because it has no way to follow the thread through the leather. Regular sewing machines work with two threads, but each returns to its own side of the material once it has looped around its partner. The technique may sound simple in the abstract, but producing tiny, identical stitches in thick leather is not easy. And hundreds of them bind a briefcase together.

ABOVE: Making the handle is often the most demanding part of a bag's construction, given the layers of leather and the functionality required.

OPPOSITE: The key element that differentiates a hand-sewn bag is the saddle stitch, where two needles are passed through a hole simultaneously. Here, it is being used to stitch together a handle.

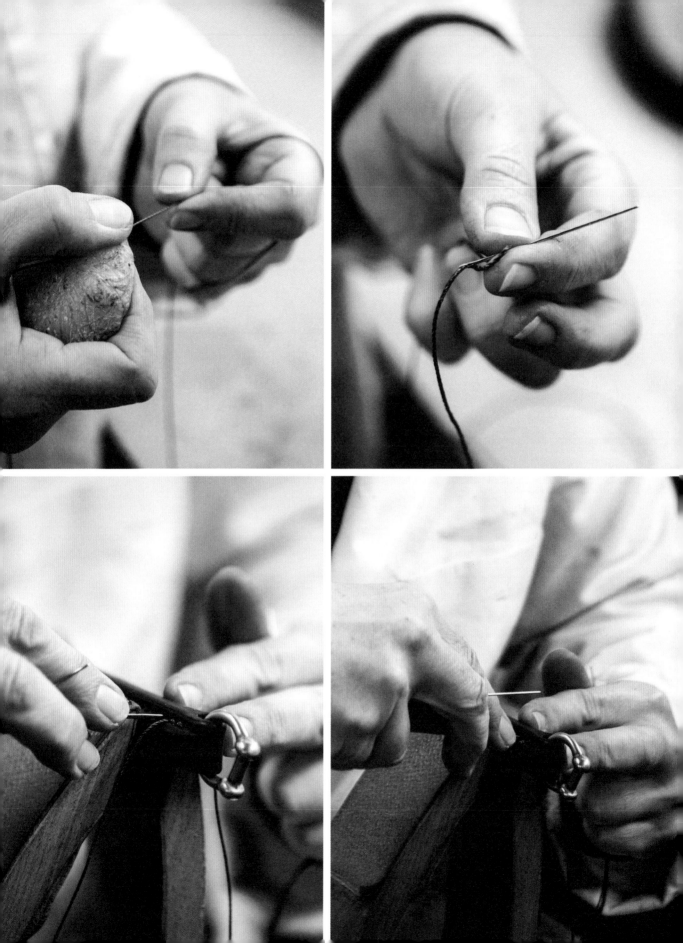

The second skill, inking, produces a rounded finish to every edge of the case. It is instantly identifiable by its smoothness. Cheaper bags finish each piece of leather individually, which means there will always be a line – and a weak point – up the centre of each join. Hand-inking involves painting the edge with a special dye, particular to the colour of the case, using a small brush. A heated iron is then used to smooth the edges and help the dye penetrate. The result is sanded down and wax is applied with the same iron. Sometimes a rag will be rubbed along the edge to melt the wax together with a little friction. Each edge requires several iterations of this process, depending on the thickness and type of leather and the number of layers. The thickest, on the edge of a handle, can take hours to complete. This handle construction is one of the oldest techniques practised at the Walthamstow factory, and probably the element that modern bags have most in common with original Dunhill models from the first half of the 20th century. That history, along with the singular vision of its founder, is one of the things that distinguishes Dunhill from other, younger purveyors of luxury accessories.

ABOVE: The panel of a bag is measured and checked.

LEFT AND OPPOSITE: Great care is taken with the leather. Although it is often cowhide, exotics and suedes are also used.

The history, the innovator

Alfred Dunhill was a man of luxury. Not in the sense of extravagance or opulence, but in his restless pursuit of quality. It is no coincidence that many of the names that survived as global luxury groups – Coco Chanel, Louis Vuitton, Thierry Hermès – had similar passions. He inherited his father's saddlery business in 1891 and used the leather traditions at the company to make accessories for the growing world of automobiles. As the products proved popular, and Alfred expanded into vehicles and then tobacco pipes, other companies consistently fought over price and sought efficiencies in their production. Alfred took the opposite course. He demanded the highest quality, invented continuously to be ahead of the market, and charged a lot more. He proved that people would pay for the best.

Alfred had so many ideas that he eventually established Alfred Dunhill's Patent Development Company to process and commercialize the intellectual property. Not all the results were motoring necessities – one Dunhill catalogue stretched to 192 pages and 1,457 items including motoring coats in pleated tweed, white sealskin, Russian foal-skin and Siberian wolf. It wasn't entirely obvious which coats were necessary for which endeavours or types of motoring.

After a brief attempt at retirement, Alfred opened a new shop in St James's, selling a range of men's accessories with a new emphasis on tobacco. During the inter-war years he continued to innovate and bring quality to ever-expanding ranges of products, from timepieces to lighters, fountain pens to make-up sets. The Art Deco ranges of lighters and related accessories are objects of peerless beauty. Understandably, demand for luxury smoking paraphernalia has died off in recent years and Dunhill's range of goods has also slimmed down considerably. Its London-made bags, however, remain a shining beacon of quality and craftsmanship at the company.

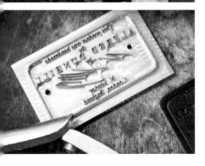

ABOVE: Alfred Dunhill stamps are prepared, ready to brand the bags.

OPPOSITE: A finished product – a London Tradition double briefcase. Note the angle and texture of the stitches, showing the handwork.

KAPITAL
THE FINEST JEANS
IN THE WORLD

DYE-HARD DENIM

THERE ARE HUNDREDS OF PURIST
DENIM COMPANIES TODAY, EACH
WITH THEIR OWN PREFERENCES
AND PRIORITIES. KAPITAL IS DOING
EVERYTHING ITSELF, AND USING THAT
FREEDOM TO EXPERIMENT.

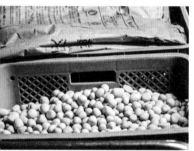

ABOVE AND BELOW: Kapital is particularly known for its washing techniques, with machines shown above and below and stones above.

OPPOSITE: Patchwork and repairs are key to the design aesthetic.

Denim attracts enthusiasts like no other aspect of menswear. It is a straightforward material, made into a narrow range of garments, yet, partly because jeans are so central to modern masculinity, denim is the subject of intense, microscopic debate. Those enthusiasts agree on more things than they may admit. They agree, for example, on the importance of quality at every stage of the denim process, from the cotton to the dyeing, the spinning to the cutting. Yet the industry is not vertically integrated. Most jeans-makers buy in their denim, the top end coming from Cone Mills in North Carolina or various mills around the Okayama area of Japan. A large part of the quality is left to somebody else.

One reason Kapital is featured here is because it is one of the few denim producers that does its own dyeing, spinning, weaving and making. It does not use the manual looms so favoured by some denim fans, but then the nature of Kapital's weaving means that the volume and, thus, the availability for the customer is very restricted.

The other reason for its inclusion is Kapital's consistent innovation. When Kazuhiro Hirata joined the company that his father Toshikiyo founded in 1984, he tore apart the model book and began to design from scratch. Some of the interwoven, washed and painted jeans that resulted may not be to sartorial tastes, but there are many subtle additions too, and innovative construction techniques that lead to some beautiful, simple and fantastically made jeans.

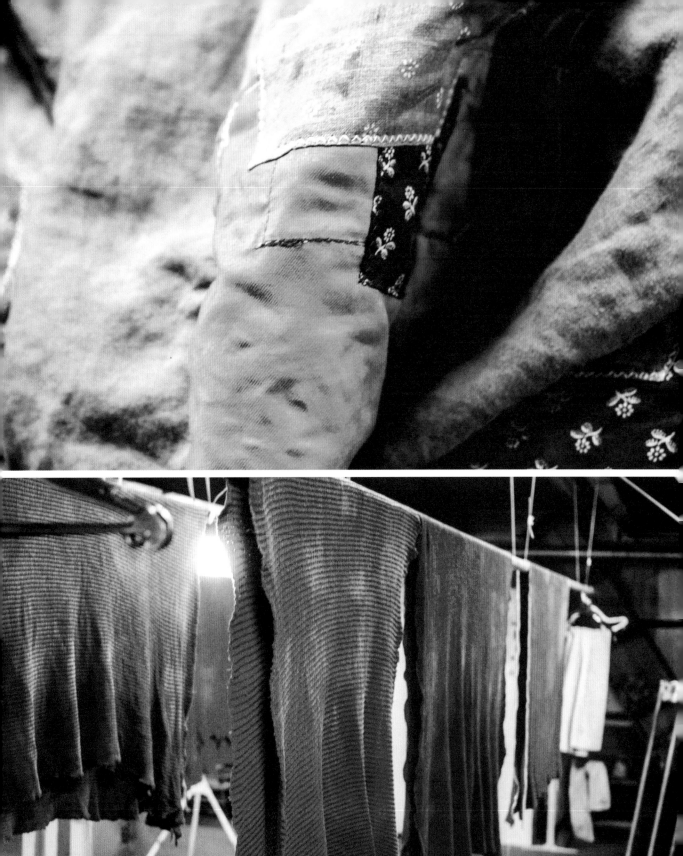

'The merit of doing everything ourselves can be summed up in one word: freedom. The freedom to change any part of the process, to challenge the assumptions in the industry,' says Toshikiyo. 'It makes it easy for us to find weaknesses, improve on them, and then experiment with little things that have perhaps a 1% chance of success. It makes innovation possible.'

American, but better

On the front of Kapital's Kountry factory there is a large picture of a raccoon. 'Every wash guaranteed!' says the poster, offering washing for 'overalls and pants'. The raccoon himself is wearing a natty pair of royal-blue dungarees. 'It stands for our ability to wash anything, just like a raccoon does,' explains Toshikiyo.

He started in the denim industry in 1975 and set up his own company a decade later. The company began its life making jeans for other brands as a so-called OEM (original equipment manufacturer) and only subsequently developed its own products. The Kountry factory, which opened in 2010 to work exclusively on washing techniques, was the first sign of expansion in Kapital's manufacturing.

Toshikiyo's motivation to found his own company came when he visited the US in the 1980s. 'The producer I was working for was just making copies of American jeans, and I got sick of it. I set up Kapital because I wanted to make better jeans than Levi's. I deliberately never put a stitch pattern on the back pocket for that reason,' he says. (The so-called arcuate stitch on the back of Levi's is a well-known trademark for the company, and has been frequently imitated.) Although his company started as an OEM, Toshikiyo steadily became frustrated at the process: 'It began that way because we didn't have the funds to start on our own. But then a lot of the customers would find fault with natural variations in the jeans we were making, or things that were the result of the materials supplied to us. They might ship back 10% and our profit was only 15%. It wasn't worth it.'

Toshikiyo's education and innovation started early. He learned a lot while making those copies of American denim, including a familiarity with the

ABOVE: Finishing touches on shirts and jeans.

OPPOSITE: The pattern process, with workers using brown paper similar to that used in many industries, including tailoring.

ABOVE: Blue hands, with the skin dyed by the indigo in the denim, are a sign of pride among Kapital workers.

OPPOSITE: With denim, some industrial-level processes are required, particularly when creating distressed effects.

fabrics, threads and dyes, the buttons and the rivets that go into jeans – and the ways that corners could be cut. On the construction side, he learned about the latest looms and sewing machines, the needles, turbines and motors, but also how some of those newer machines produced lower-quality jeans because of the scale of their production.

When he set up Kapital as an OEM, Toshikiyo developed a new sewing technique that enabled the stitching of thicker fabrics. This came in useful when Kapital began making its own product, working with thicker yarn and older looms that combined to make a heavier, more substantial denim.

Proud of our blue hands

Good denim starts with the raw material – long staple cotton. It then has to be gravity spun, to make the yarn, and dyed. Kapital is one of the very few denim producers to mix their own dyes, using different combinations of natural indigos to create subtly different colours. Indigo No. 1 and No. 2 were created when Kapital started, the first intended to resemble American vintage wear and the second a deeper, more Japanese blue.

Best of all, though, is the Saitama Bushu Dye that is used in Kapital's skein dyeing. Standard cottons are rope-dyed – the yarn is stretched out like a rope and dipped into the dye. This leaves colour on the outside but the core of the thread is white, hence its name in Japanese: *nakashiro*, or inner white.

With skein dyeing, the thread is bundled up and dipped into the dye, left for 24 hours, taken out and cleaned, and then dipped again, 12 to 13 times. It also requires careful adjustment depending on the season, the temperature and humidity. The result is a much richer blue, with the thread dyed to its core. 'The care we take in this dyeing process is why the symbol of Kapital is two blue hands,' says Kazuhiro. 'Our craftsmen take pride in the blue staining that covers their hands, their arms and their clothes.'

The beauty of good indigo emerges slowly over the life of a pair of jeans, as they are worn and fade in a pattern determined by the wearer, his physicality and habits. This is one of the lovely things about well-dyed cotton, and

something often not appreciated by fans of the leather patina on bags, jackets and shoes. It is also hard to replicate. While aged leather can work quite well, artificially faded jeans always look, well, artificial.

The problem with selvedge

The weaving of denim is pretty straightforward. The only important thing for quality is to use a smaller and less-automated loom, so that attention can be paid to the cloth as it is woven. With a loom that is small (up to 36 inches wide) and manual or semi-automatic, the weaver can watch the cloth, see when slubs (little imperfections in the cloth) are produced and lock them down, retaining the character of the material. An automatic loom, moving much faster and up to seven metres wide, will simply rip out the slub and start weaving again. And only narrower looms can use the rougher, gravity-spun thread.

It's worth noting that selvedge – long a sign of quality in jeans – is not the guarantee it once was. Selvedge is the coloured strip that runs down the edge of the denim cloth. Because the edge is stronger, the jeans should be stronger too. Today, however, many looms can produce selvedge in the middle of cloth, so its role has been undermined.

After weaving comes the cutting of the denim. As with the weaving, the important thing is to work with the cloth. Too many manufacturers stamp the patterns without considering the best positions for each section. Then, finally, there are the rivets. These are quite standard, though Kapital does occasionally use pure gold or silver rivets.

'Everything we do has a purpose, a reason and a story behind it,' says Kazuhiro. 'Even though a lot of the details aren't visible when you initially compare the denim, they come through over time as they are worn.'

ABOVE AND OPPOSITE: Each worker has their own dedicated area where they assemble the jeans, often using vintage sewing machines. Below, sample patchworks are analysed for possible future products.

Looms as war reparations

Okayama has long been the centre of denim production in Japan. The region particularly benefited from a US programme after the end of the Second World War that gave tax breaks to American manufacturers if they sent machinery to Japan. Many fabric producers sent their old, narrow looms, which fitted nicely into Japan's traditional garage industry.

Many Americans thought this was great: they could be paid for their rubbish. They weren't laughing, though, when Japan became the leading producer of high-quality denim – Levi's even tried to buy some back in the 1980s, but everyone said no. 'I love that garage mentality in Japan,' comments Neil Christopher of British workwear specialist ARN Mercantile. 'I know a guy who makes windscreen wipers for Honda in his garage.'

Okayama had been making clothing long before this influx of machinery. Ever since the Meiji Restoration in 1868, the Kojima area that sits on the southern tip of Okayama had been known for textiles, due to its pioneering use of *momen* – soaked mulberry bark fibres – to make traditional Japanese socks, or *tabi*. When demand for the socks fell, the area diversified into school uniforms (still using the *momen*) and jeans, among other things. Kojima became known as the 'capital' of Japanese denim production – hence the Kapital name.

The company now has three factories: 'Kapital' in Kojima, the 'Mitsu' factory in northern Okayama that produces most of the denim, and the 'Kountry' factory mentioned earlier, which takes care of washes and special treatments. Around 200 workers across the three locations produce just over 3,000 pairs of jeans a year.

But it is Kojima that Kazuhiro and Toshikiyo talk about most: the little town nestling on the coast, visible from the Great Seto Bridge (one of the longest in the world) that runs above it, connecting the mainland with Shikoku island. Kapital set up its first shop in Kojima in 1995 and although it now has 16 across Japan, that shop and the factory down the road remain the heart of the company.

ABOVE AND OPPOSITE: Jeans drying, always straight and always inside out.

KITON
THE FINEST SHIRTS
IN THE WORLD

CONTROL FREAKS

KITON HAS A NEAR-OBSESSIVE ATTENTION TO QUALITY AND CONSISTENCY, HAND-SEWING EVERY ASPECT OF ITS SHIRTS AND INVENTING ENTIRELY NEW TECHNIQUES.

Kiton does great mozzarella. Granted, any local Italian mozzarella is a revelation to an Englishman brought up on exports, but the starter in Kiton's dining hall was particularly delicious. Just a drizzle of extra virgin olive oil, with sliced beef tomatoes and fresh bread. Then fresh fish, brought out by a jocular chef. Both the staff and the chef have been at Kiton a long time.

Management eat last, so the hall, which seats 200, was almost empty by the time we sat down for lunch at the kitchen end, just 20 of us enjoying what was the third sitting. Down below, through the frosted glass, tailors and cutters were already returning to their posts, pulling off basted jackets from a pile. Those doing the hand-sewing of collars, sleeves and buttonholes sat in circles, their feet propped against a low table between them, working on their knees.

Kiton is a special company – and not because of the shared dining, the quality of the food or the communal atmosphere. These things might be alien to an English or American business, but they are common among Italian luxury manufacturers. You'll find a similar set-up at Zegna, Pal Zileri or Canali. Kiton is unique because of the amount of product it makes itself.

Control leads to quality

When Kiton wanted to expand into sportswear, it bought what it considered to be the best sportswear company in Italy, including a knitwear facility that supplies many of the world's luxury names, such as Hermès. It bought the company because it wanted to control production. For that reason, as much else as possible is made on the same site, in a complex of buildings just outside Naples. When I last visited they had just completed a new, third building. The tie-making and shoemaking had moved in and the fledgling tailoring school was getting used to its new space on the ground floor.

This fixation on control comes across clearly in the way some products are cut. The silk to make the ties, for example, is cut one square at a time. As explained in the chapter on Drake's ties, this individual cutting doesn't make any difference to quality, but Kiton does it because it allows individual shop managers around the world to order just a few ties to particular specifications, or to have bespoke ties made quickly for their clients.

ABOVE: Kiton hand-cuts every one of its shirts, even those readymade to standard sizes.

OPPOSITE: Cardboard templates are used to mark out the panels of the shirt on a long cutting table.

The cotton for the shirts is cut one piece at a time too, as is the wool for the suits even if the cutter has to make a dozen 38Rs in a row. It is better to cut suit cloth one piece at a time, but this is only partly why Kiton works this way. The individual cutting also allows Riccardo Renzi, manager of the London store, to have his 38Rs cut a little longer in the body, with a slightly larger sleevehead to exaggerate the *spalla camicia* effect (the 'shirt shoulder', where the sleeve of the suit runs underneath the shoulder panel, in the same way a shirt is made). Riccardo knows what his customers like. He is also the only store manager to stock one-piece ties – that's one piece of wool or silk, from end to end of the tie, folded in on itself seven times. They may be extremely expensive, but Riccardo has the clients who want them: the kind of man who seeks an individual and almost extravagant demonstration of craft.

The best shirts

This approach reaches perhaps its greatest expression in the company's approach to shirts. During the making of a Kiton shirt only two elements are done on a sewing machine: the outer edges of the collars and cuffs (so as to present a cleaner, sharper line at the neck and wrist); and the seams of the body, sleeves and armholes (for strength). On the side seams, however, the machine-stitching is followed by hand-stitching. Someone folds the edge of the shirt over and sews it up by hand, which allows the shirt body to move more easily and makes it less likely to stretch permanently. The machine stitch is merely a back-up to keep the parts together.

Most shirts use two lines of machine stitching on the side seams. This creates a little ridge of cloth that is less comfortable than a hand-sewn finish. Some, mostly French, makers emphasize the number of (machine) stitches to the inch. They say this increases longevity and gives a finer appearance to the shirt, but I've never had a machine-sewn shirt even threaten to come undone at the seams. Hand-stitching is both prettier and more comfortable.

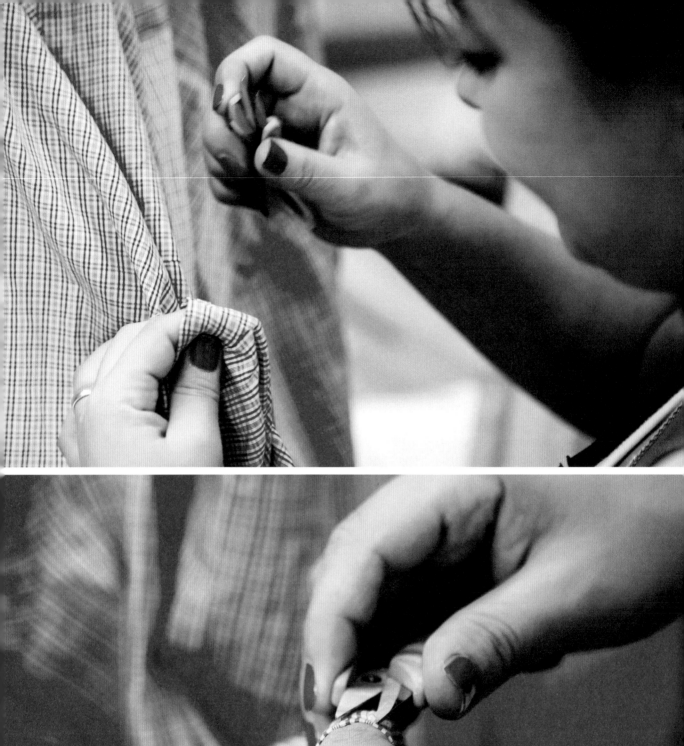
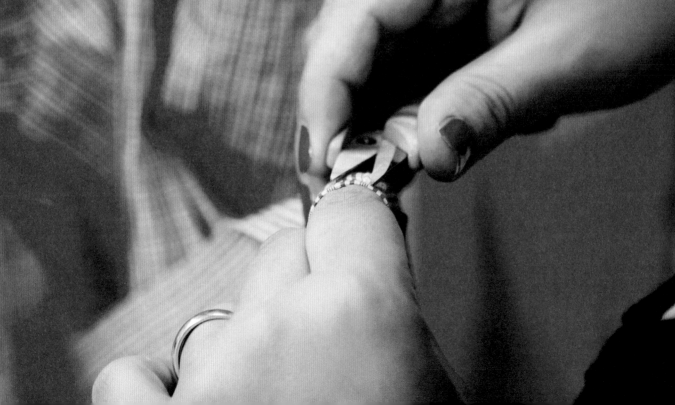

Finished like a handkerchief

The bottom edge of a Kiton shirt is entirely finished by hand, being turned over like a hand-rolled handkerchief. The cuff is attached by hand, gradually easing in the fullness of the sleeve (though some are also folded in pleats, if the customer or store prefers). The sleeve is attached similarly, the fullness here being particularly important to give greatest freedom of movement – anyone with even a passing acquaintance with bespoke tailoring knows the importance of a small armhole and a large sleevehead. Interestingly, the Kiton shirtmakers insist on the sleeve being set into the body so that its seam runs slightly in front of the body's side seam. Look in the armpit of any normal shirt and you'll see these two seams line up. It's a lot easier to make that way. But Sebastiano Borrelli, head of the shirtmaking department at Kiton, insists that this way is a more natural setting for the sleeve. 'It pitches the sleeve forward from the body, as your arms naturally fall. No one's arms fall straight down at their sides,' he explains. 'Having the seams aligned differently also enables the rotation of the sleeve to be different, so its seam is further upwards and less likely to be pressed on, when you rest your arm, for instance.'

The collar is what you notice

I own several Kiton shirts and they are amazingly comfortable. It's hard to know, though, whether it's down to the stunning quality of the cotton or tailoring aspects. One immediately obvious benefit, however, is attaching the collar to the body of the shirt by hand. It is worked by upturning the collar and sticking it to the body with a pin, then buttoning the collar closed. The tailor then sews it onto the shirt, which means the shirt collar retains its shape even when unbuttoned.

ABOVE AND OPPOSITE: Quality control is central to the Kiton production process, with workers snipping off any excess threads.

Other interesting details are that Kiton uses no interlining down the placket of their shirts, which is actually cheaper but makes them lighter to wear. The placket is basted back onto the shirt by hand. All the buttonholes are sewn by hand, which seems like an awful lot of effort even to someone used to closely examining the buttonholes on his suits. The buttons are also sewn on by hand, using the 'chicken foot' or three-pointed technique to show it off. And, finally, the collar is an interesting mix of fused and floating construction, with a light, floating canvas throughout for comfort but fused sections at both ends to keep them sharper. This was an innovation of Sebastiano Borrelli's.

As his name suggests, Sebastiano is a scion of the famous Borrelli shirtmaking family. So how was he tempted away to a Neapolitan competitor? 'It was an encounter with Ciro Paone [Kiton's founder],' Sebastiano recalls. 'He said to me, "how do you make the best shirts in the world?" After some discussion of technique and manufacture he declared, "I want you to set up a shirtmaking department for me. You will have complete freedom to do whatever you want; cost is not an object. Just make the best shirts possible".'

That kind of offer is inspiring, but it also brings a sense of responsibility: 'I remember that always, that desire and trust in me,' Sebastiano says. 'It's what drives me to innovate constantly.'

Many Neapolitan shirts include hand-sewing, where English shirts at the same price would not. Borrelli shirts are a good example and very good value for the amount of handwork they require. So Kiton is not alone. But Kiton is pretty much the only international brand to offer shirts with all these steps, with every working aspect being sewn by hand – and is constantly setting itself apart through its innovation. You can't help feeling a lot of it is down to focus, control, and having everyone fed on lovely local cheese.

RIGHT: Shirts are pressed ready to be packaged for stores.

LORO PIANA

THE FINEST KNITWEAR IN THE WORLD

A QUEST FOR THE BEST

MANY THINGS SET LORO PIANA APART FROM ITS PEERS, INCLUDING SCALE, QUALITY AND INNOVATION. BUT THE MOST IMPORTANT – CERTAINLY FOR KNITWEAR – IS VERTICAL INTEGRATION.

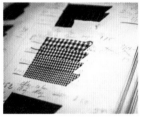

Loro Piana sources all its own raw materials, so the rarest and most luxurious fabrics always find their way into the Loro Piana collection first – only later trickling down into the mainstream. The company became the exclusive purveyor of vicuña for a decade. Baby cashmere and cloth from the lotus flower were a result of restless exploration by Pier-Luigi Loro Piana. The first discovery, however, was by Pier-Luigi's father, Franco Loro Piana, in the 1950s.

The family had been wool traders for generations, going back to the early 19th century. In 1924, Franco's uncle Pietro Loro Piana set up the first family company to sell woollen cloth (the cloth division of the company still bears his name). It wasn't, however, until international travel became easier that Franco began travelling and bringing back both mechanical innovations and new wools.

The stand-out success was Tasmanian: a 2-by-1 cloth made from merino wool that Franco bought in Australia. '2-by-1' refers to the innovative weaving pattern, with two threads in the warp to only one in the weft (cloth had previously all been 2-by-2). This lighter weave made Tasmanian the first four-season cloth, which could be worn almost all year round in Italy. It was markedly different from the heavy English woollens that dominated much of the market. 'It was a phenomenal success, selling millions of metres soon after launch and is still a best-seller today,' says Pier-Luigi. 'Tasmanian was probably the world's first branded cloth. Men used to keep the labels on the outside of the jacket cuff, to show off what it was made of.'

In the 1980s, Loro Piana was the first company to bring cashmere back from Mongolia itself, establishing relationships with the local producers, which enabled the company to control the quality more effectively. Today, Loro Piana is still the only brand that works in Mongolia on this individual level, with its own local trading company. Outside the trading company's tent there is a sign that says 'We buy cashmere 24 hours'. Herdsmen trust it over other traders because of its long-standing relationships (and electronic scales).

The lengths we go to

The next first came in Peru, where for many years it had been illegal to sell vicuña. The camelid the wool comes from had been hunted to near extinction – a long decline that began with the import of rifles by the Spanish. By 1950, there were only 6,000 vicuñas left. Both Franco and Pier-Luigi had known about the legendary material, which was so soft only the king of the Incas was allowed to wear it (woven with gold, and discarded at the end of each day), but had been unable to import it.

Then in the 1980s, Loro Piana began working with the Peruvian government to help the numbers recover, bringing in fences, breeding expertise and advice on how to harvest the wool without killing the animal – which had been normal practice until then. As a result, the company won an exclusive contract to buy and sell vicuña for ten years, from 1994 to 2004. Even today, Loro Piana buys the majority of the annual production.

Baby cashmere was the next innovation, following a long campaign by Pier-Luigi in Mongolia. He found that the underhair of hircus goats in their first year was a good degree finer than adult cashmere – around 13 microns as opposed to 15. Normally the nomadic herdsmen would put all cashmere into the same delivery – it was enough of an effort just to separate the soft underhair from the coarser body hair of the goat, and Loro Piana had exacting standards.

But gradually they were persuaded to sell baby cashmere separately, for a higher price. Again, for a long time Loro Piana was the only company selling the material, and still has the vast bulk of world supply.

The latest discovery is cloth woven from the filaments of the lotus flower. And it is this story that demonstrates the primacy of innovation and exploration at Loro Piana. Pier-Luigi travelled to Myanmar, where the cloth is produced, many times before he was able to source any of the material. After five years, he established a small group of women who could weave 40 metres a month on the old wooden looms used locally. Two years later, the company offered its first product – a run of 150 jackets.

ABOVE: Cloth races out of the high-speed looms, but often has to wait for several careful finishing processes.

OPPOSITE: One of the most important stages in production is quality control, where stray threads are removed and – occasionally – have to be rewoven back into the cloth. This is a painstaking process, but can save cloth worth thousands of euros.

The quality and the control

Since Loro Piana started selling clothes rather than just cloth in 1994, revenue has increased rapidly, culminating in the sale of an 80% stake to LVMH for two billion euros in 2013. It has grown from two stores in Milan and Venice in 1998 to over a hundred today. It is a giant.

You get a sense of that size, as well as the inevitable results of consistent experimentation, in the stock room. Based in Loro Piana's Quarona headquarters, which house the weaving, finishing and quality control, the room's scale is astonishing. It is filled with 5,000 small grey crates, each of which contains a dozen or so cones of yarn, classified by their purpose and date of creation. The shelves, 30 or 40 crates high, recede into a blurry vanishing point from the viewing gallery halfway up one wall. The only other occupant of the room is a scuttling robot that whizzes up and down, out and back, fetching crates requested by the designers. It is an industrial sorting office for 250,000 kilos of cashmere.

Down the road in Sillavengo this wool is turned into knitwear. Cones of cashmere are trucked down the road to this small, one-storey building where around a dozen knitting machines produce the individual panels that make up Loro Piana sweaters. Like any quality knitwear, Loro Piana's is fully fashioned, meaning that the back, front and sleeves are knitted to size rather than being cut out of a larger piece of cloth.

One advantage of Loro Piana's vertical integration and piece-by-piece production is that it can produce made-to-measure knitwear relatively inexpensively (it costs the customer about 20% more than the standard off-the-shelf sweater).

ABOVE: Samples of yarn are accessed in Loro Piana's vast storage facility; old, used teasels are discarded.

OPPOSITE: Teasels (dried plant heads) are still the most effective way of combing the surface of the finest materials.

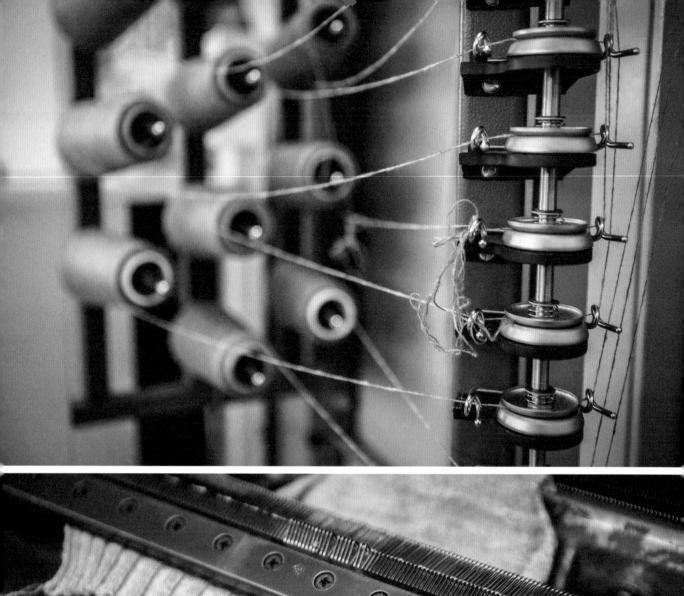

Made-to-measure knitwear is something that Loro Piana is beginning to promote more heavily, recognizing that customers looking for the best knitwear in the world – and who are possibly already clients of a bespoke tailor – want a perfect fit as well as a perfect make.

'With everything we do, we are aiming to fit into our customers' lifestyle, their needs and desires. Bespoke and personalized items are definitely a growth area and something we are looking to expand,' says Pier-Luigi.

The modern aesthetic

Loro Piana sources the best materials and uses the best production techniques. But, crucially, it also has the design expertise to apply to both. Pier-Luigi admits that this was a concern when the new readymade line was launched in 1994. The company's history was in cloth, not fashion, and it was entering a crowded market for luxury Italian clothing. Anyone who visits the Pitti Uomo menswear trade shows in Florence will be aware of quite how many Italian brands there are offering the same grey cashmere and brown suede aesthetic. In a few short years, Loro Piana has become the paradigm of that Italian off-duty look. Its 'Roadster' pullover has become a modern classic, the zip-up neck and full body designed for those lucky men driving their open-top sports cars around Italy's mountain roads. The 'Horsey' jacket,

ABOVE: Cardboard patterns, each panel representing a part of the finished piece of knitwear.

OPPOSITE: A series of different lighted surfaces are used to check the knitwear, including pairs of vertical tubes that can be inserted into the sleeves.

designed for the Italian Olympic show-jumping team, is another staple
and the Storm System waterproof treatment it uses has been patented and
widely licensed.

Loro Piana has reached the zenith of quality in many areas, from leather
jackets to suede slip-ons. But knitwear remains at the company's heart, largely
because of its roots in raw materials.

'Baby cashmere, vicuña, the finest wools are the cornerstone of what we
do – and so it is natural that everything in the readymade collection begins with
knitwear,' says Pier-Luigi.

RIGHT: The finished product, a cream baby-cashmere
V-neck that was made to measure for the author.

OPPOSITE: A close-up of the neckline shows the subtle
melange of colours.

MARIO TALARICO

THE FINEST UMBRELLAS
IN THE WORLD

KNOBS AND KNOBBLY WOODS
A SMALL WORKSHOP WITH A GROWING INTERNATIONAL FOLLOWING, MARIO TALARICO MAKES WHOLE-STICK UMBRELLAS OUT OF A BEAUTIFUL RANGE OF VARIEGATED WOODS.

Naples may have a reputation for dirt and danger, but developments such as the promenade that faces onto the Mediterranean are turning it, ever so slowly, into a modern tourist destination. If there were a street where danger would lurk, however, it would be Vico Due Porte – a tiny street off the main shopping strip of Via Toledo. It is narrow, and dark as a result, with the apartments above hanging over the shops and further closing out the sunlight. Being at the foot of a steep hill means light is blocked off on a third side too, leaving only a few rays of light to filter in at the Toledo entrance. Even a local taxi driver will take several false turns before he can find it. Yet this is the location of perhaps the best umbrella-maker in the world.

Steeped in history

Mario Talarico is part of a family tradition that goes back to 1860. But as with many storied manufacturers, that doesn't mean that Talarico has been making great umbrellas for 150 years. For a long time, the family was just one of many in Naples making umbrellas. They made them by hand because there were no machines to help. Then, for a period, the quality fell when there seemed to be no demand. Why hand-sew the protective covers around the hinges when nobody cares, when all they want is to pay as little as possible?

OPPOSITE: Mario Talarico is part of a long family tradition of umbrella-making in Naples. In recent years, he has taken to producing the finest examples in the city.

The quality has come back up in the last decade. There are now mother-of-pearl buttons on the closures throughout. The rings that fasten to those buttons are sewn all around, to prevent any chafing. The relatively recent nature of this improvement may explain why the Talarico shop-front is so off-putting. It is dominated by cheap umbrellas in bright, plastic colours. They are short, hand-held and include cartoon-character motifs. Yours for ten euros. There isn't a huge demand for umbrellas in Naples (the sun takes care of that) and most of the demand is for this inexpensive, disposable variety.

Increasingly, though, the Talarico reputation for quality is spreading. So gentlemen will venture inside, let their eyes adjust to the duller shade of canopy on display and ask about the Malacca handles, or the chestnut with that special ruddy glow.

They gaze in awe at Mario's desk, which he says is over 200 years old. It is worn away to a remarkable degree, with a chunk taken out of the front that suggests a furious shark bite. Other parts just look melted. When Mario sits at it, nestled into the bitten-off space, he hunches over his work. The shelves are close above his head. Indeed, it's hard to know which came first – the shelves or the hunch – but the two fit together as neatly as puzzle pieces.

My favourite part of this hermit's cave is the drawers. Starting on those shoulder-high shelves, they run in several rows along the wall, each overflowing with the different parts required in the trade: tacks, screws, metal wire. The wood is worn smooth through use. Labels are yellowed and curling. Sitting just below them, behind Mario, is a bench drill. This is used to bore a hole in the end of the wooden shaft, so a tip can be attached – usually buffalo horn, as it is much more resistant than wood and just as attractive (certainly more so than the normal metal tips).

The same machinery is used for polishing, with buffalo horn taking the most work. A handle made of horn begins as five or six rough brown chunks. By polishing them down to a fine shine and carefully matching the colours, you can give the impression of a one-piece horn handle – only hairlines betray the joins.

ABOVE: The drawers around Mario's desk contain tacks, screws, buttons and other useful parts.

OPPOSITE: Polishing equipment, and Mario's 200-year-old desk.

A beautiful length of wood

Most connoisseurs dislike such decorative handles, however, because the central craft of making an umbrella is manipulating a beautiful piece of wood into a shaft and handle combined. It is far easier to have a separate handle and shaft – one straight piece, one curved piece – than to take a length of wood, soak it until it becomes malleable and then, over a period of days, force the grain gradually into a curve. Some woods are more difficult than others, but pushing any wood into more than a 180-degree turn is tough.

What's more, the wood must be the perfect width for the shaft (it cannot be shaved down if the features of the surface are to be retained), with a characterful knob at one end to finish off the handle. This is often the most beautiful part of the umbrella: the polished, bulbous end that shows off both the interior of the wood and the layers of grain. After the shaft is ready, two more stages are required: sinking the metal, mechanical pieces into the shaft and sewing a canopy. The canopy will be secured when closed by a ring just below the rosette (the central mechanism from which the arms radiate), hooking onto a triangle attached to the wood. Mario does this by hand, cutting into the wood and slotting in a piece of wire he has bent. There is no advantage to doing this by hand rather than in a mechanized process, but it is easier to adapt to particularly tricky or knobbly woods.

The final stage is the sewing of the canopy. Mario uses treated cotton, with a variety of colours and patterns. Silk is more traditional for a business umbrella and more common in countries such as the UK, but it makes for a much sleeker appearance that is not suited to most of the rustic woods Mario uses. As Mario Junior says: 'A silk umbrella is a sword; these are clubs.'

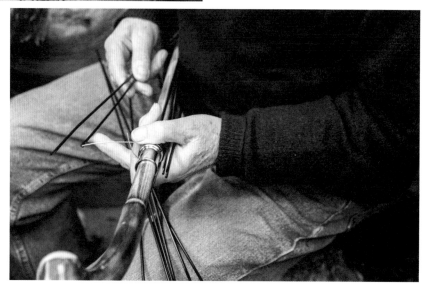

ABOVE AND OPPOSITE: The arms of the umbrella are fixed into the
rosette, the metal collar that allows the umbrella to expand and contract.

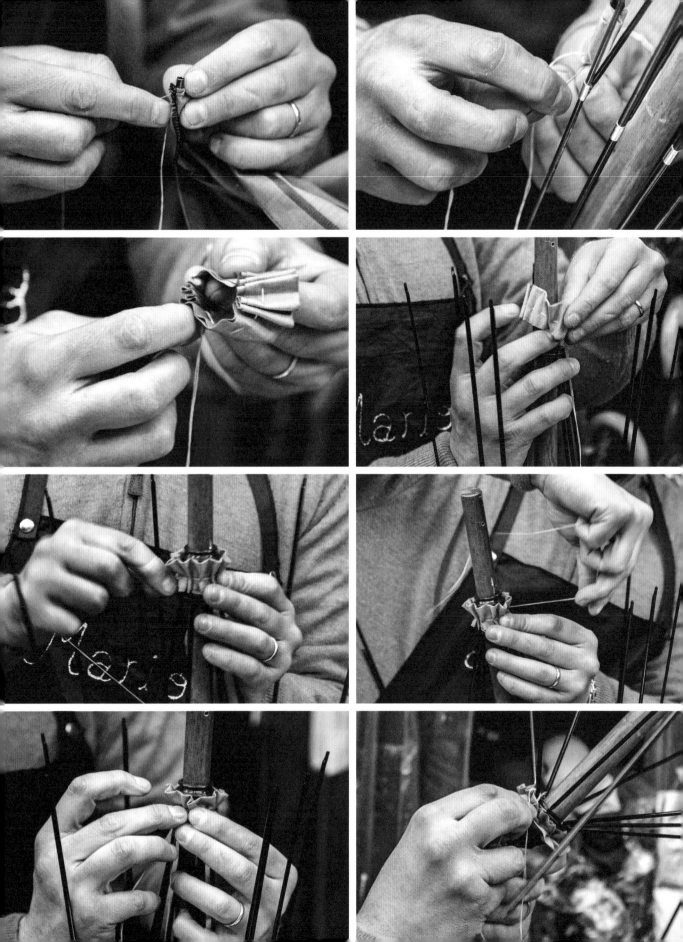

Junior takes over

Before the canopy can be attached, though, small strips of the same cloth must be sewn around the interior hinges – including the rosette. I watched Mario Junior do this (he's actually Mario's nephew) behind the glass-topped shop counter. A young man with a passion for the craft, he hates doing repairs – the creativity of constructing a new piece is his big love.

Junior cuts the strips by eye from spare cloth left over from the canopy. He winds a strip around the hinge and then stitches it into place, going around the arm of the frame four or five times. The process is repeated on each arm, before moving onto the slightly more complicated protection for the rosette. It is fiddly because the thread must be looped in and out of each of the arms, but that means it can't be replicated by a machine.

Junior also paints on the umbrellas. An umbrella with a painted horse on it may not be to everyone's taste, but there is clearly a demand for them and Mario Junior's work is lovely. Indeed, he illustrated a special white umbrella that was given to Pope John Paul II when he visited Naples. A photograph commemorating the occasion hangs above the counter.

This is a good excuse to mention the rest of the photographs. There are scores of them, stuck to the walls, hanging from the ceiling and pressed under the counter-top. They show the elder Mario with politicians (Italian and international), film stars and fashion designers. Fendi, in particular, has always been a big supporter of Mario and his work and there are three pictures of him with the Fendi sisters. Not recognizing them initially, I ask him whether one of them is his wife: he sits up, smiles wryly and hunches back over his desk.

ABOVE: Mario Junior at work, surrounded by finished products and photographs of famous customers.

OPPOSITE: Junior sews cloth around the rosette, weaving the thread in and out of the arms.

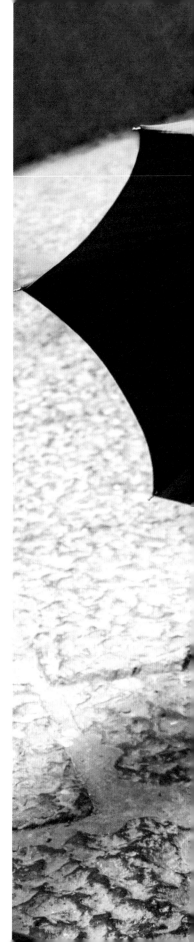

The value of a good umbrella

Men have very few accessories they can spend money on, and fewer still they can display without fear of foppishness. There is the wallet, which can be in a lovely leather and hand-sewn; there is the watch, which can be very expensive, but, like the wallet, should remain hidden most of the time; and there are odds and ends such as card cases and lighters. None of them is naturally carried, forthright, in the hand. In an age where men don't wear a hat unless it's actually freezing, the umbrella is the most demonstrative accessory.

So it's worth making it a nice one. Even the fanciest woods are rough enough to escape accusations of femininity, so go wild with knobbly chestnut and polished rosewood. There is a tradition of strong colours and colour combinations, at least outside the straight business umbrella (the sword rather than the club), so consider greens, blues or yellows.

Talarico's range includes many of these combinations. Indeed, Mario has an eye for these details that belies his stained work trousers and scruffy sweater. So while you can visit the little alley in Naples for workmanship – the single-piece shaft and hand-sewn canvas – there's a good chance you'll walk away with an umbrella because a rare wood caught your eye. And it is that combination of skills, rather than the family's 150 years of tradition, that lies behind the recommendation of Talarico as the finest source of umbrellas in the world.

RIGHT: A finished umbrella sitting outside on Vico Due Porte. The simple stick is set off by a rather more flamboyant canopy.

ZILLI

THE FINEST LEATHER
JACKETS IN THE WORLD

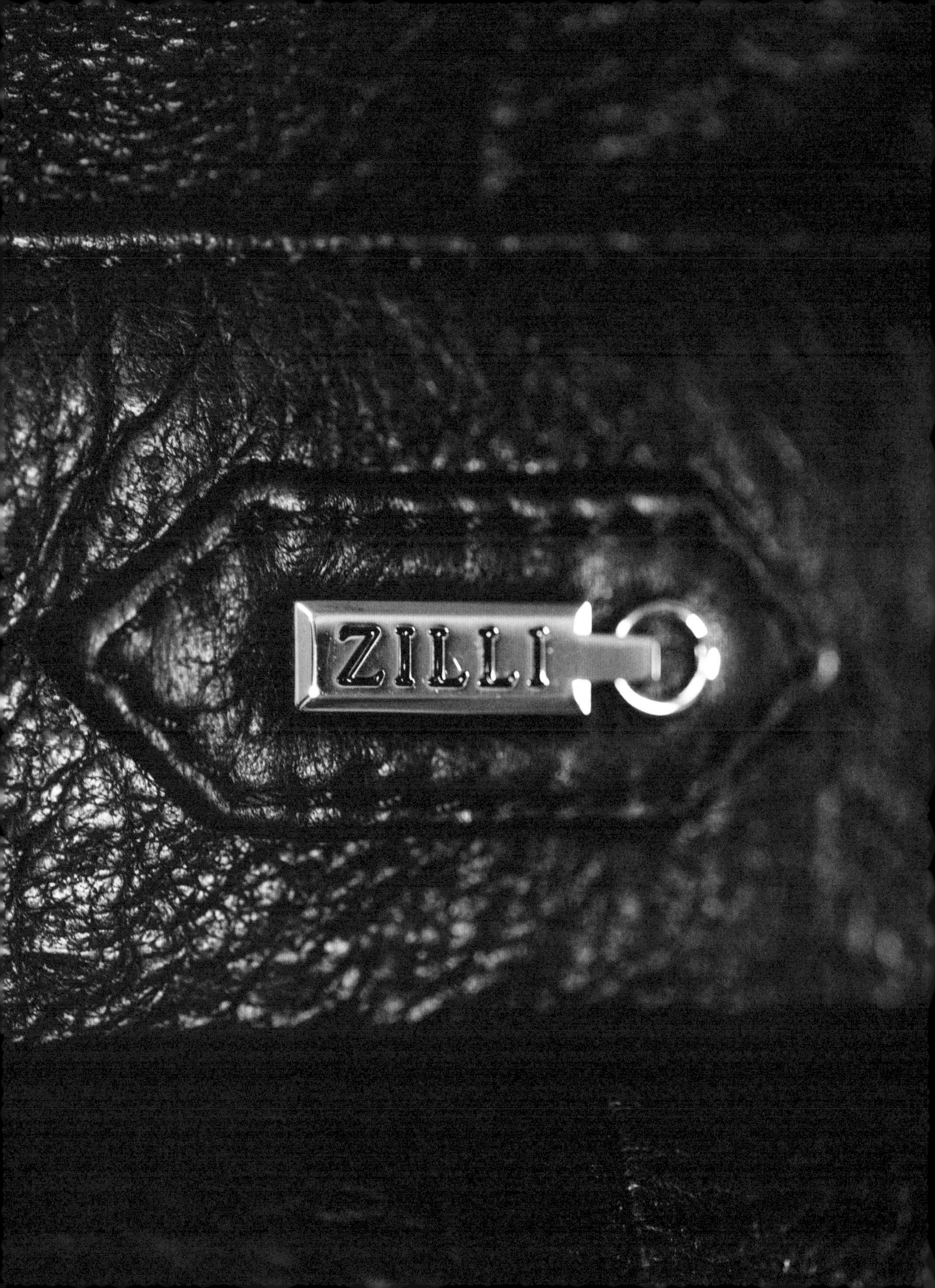
ZILLI

THE SUBSTANCE BEHIND THE STYLE

ZILLI WAS ONE OF THE FIRST COMPANIES TO BEGIN MAKING LUXURY CASUAL WEAR, PARTICULARLY LEATHER JACKETS. TODAY, IT PRODUCES SOME OF THE RAREST AND MOST LUXURIOUS JACKETS IN THE WORLD.

ABOVE, TOP: The leather facility at Zilli, up in the roof of the building.

ABOVE AND OPPOSITE: Close-ups of various skins carefully collected, analysed and used at Zilli, including peccary (opposite, bottom) complete with marks of the shot that killed it.

I've always had a thing for leather. A vast number of beasts give up their hides and because of the multifarious ways they can be treated or finished a huge variety of looks, textures and handles can be achieved. Zilli, the French luxury house based in Lyon, is known for brash styling and flashy clients. Less well known is the phenomenal quality and workmanship of its leather jackets. During a visit to their factory, I witnessed some of the devotion that goes into the procuring and preparation of the best leathers in the world.

Hides among the rafters

The third floor of the Zilli factory is large, but low-ceilinged. This probably enhances the impression of a wide space crowded with every conceivable type of leather. The back wall is mostly taken up with crocodile skins, hanging floor to ceiling and arranged in a rainbow of colours. Down the middle of the room run two long tables, with current projects ranged along them. The back right corner is dedicated to piles of tan-coloured peccary – the small, South-American pig that is one of the most malleable skins available. Along the left and right walls run metal shelves, which are mostly used to store the distinctive Zilli silks that line the jackets.

The soft, natural appearance of peccary gives it a particular appeal. Because it has to be hunted wild, each skin has a range of shot marks across it, instantly recalling the moment the animal was killed. These shot marks make it very hard to source enough hides to make a jacket: you only need about 20 skins, but that might require sourcing and checking close to 200. Unsurprisingly, therefore, Zilli is one of the few companies in the world that makes them.

Peccary demonstrates something about the philosophy at Zilli. Although the eye-watering price of a Zilli jacket covers the cost of sourcing 200 pig skins, it doesn't account for the frustrating and time-consuming process of making one. The supply is unpredictable. The manpower involved is huge. The end product is so hard-wearing that not a single one has been returned to Zilli for repair in 42 years.

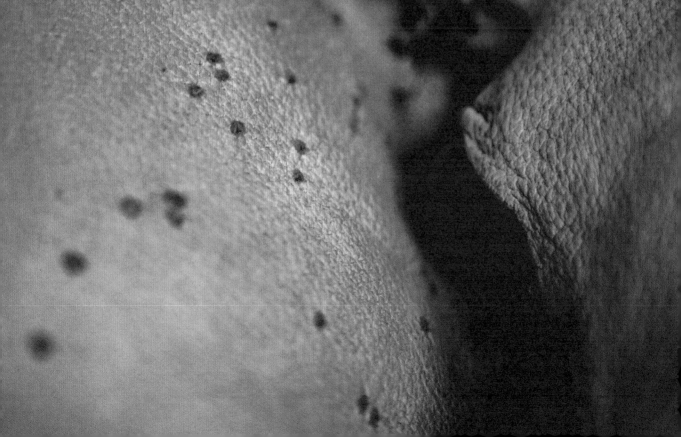

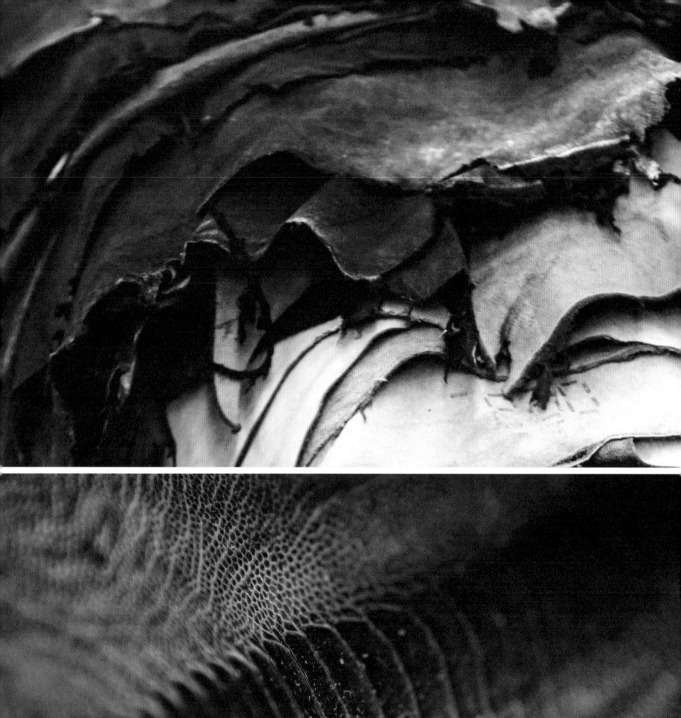

'It shares a lot of the toughness of kangaroo,' says Jean-Michel Pereira, PR and Media Manager. 'Kangaroo is often used for football boots because it is robust in the same way, yet very thin. Peccary is also tough and incredibly soft.'

You will probably have seen peccary used for gloves and small leather goods (it is not economical for most companies to make anything bigger). You can certainly recognize it easily: the skin is covered in sets of three holes, where the pig's hair follicles have been removed.

Glaze and velvet

Other distinctive Zilli leathers are velvet calf suede and glazed lambskin. The adjectives in each case are not Zilli marketing, but descriptions of the tanning process. Zilli works with a local tannery in southern France to develop new techniques for softer and thinner leathers to use in ever more luxurious jackets. The velvet calf suede feels just like the napped cotton fabric it is named after, silky smooth and soft to the touch. Glazed lambskin, on the other hand, is extremely thin and lightweight, and used to make summer jackets and those destined for the Middle Eastern or South-East Asian market.

Quality control in these leathers requires experience that comes from years of working with them up close. Joffrey de Latude, the head of the leather stock department, has been at Zilli for 18 years. There is no training programme: over time some younger staff simply develop their eye to the point that they can detect the slight imperfections and colour variations necessary to know which hides to accept and which to reject. While I was there Joffrey was sorting out a batch of glazed lambskin that was being sent back to the tannery: it was the wrong shade of navy. I couldn't see any difference from the other skins until he placed the two together and showed the slightly grey cast. 'You don't have that option with all leathers,' Joffrey said. 'Python, for example, is impossible to match up. If you look at a sheet of it, with all the long skins sewn together, each will have a slightly different tone.' He pulled out a sheet to show me the

ABOVE: Glazed lambskin piled up, and furs that have been recently dyed.

OPPOSITE: Distinguishing subtle variations in tone is one of the key skills of the leather-workers. It's only when skins are set next to each other, or examined from different angles, that such variations reveal themselves.

different casts – 'red, blue, green, purple'. As you might expect, the differences were entirely imperceptible until he pointed them out.

'The nightmare is brown calf suede because in brown you have all these colours – red, yellow, beige, even green. There's too much variation. Matching the skins across a brown suede jacket is a real feat,' Joffrey says. Because Zilli is constantly innovating, he has to come up with new standards for the fresh inventions. The way crocodile is tanned, for example, is developing all the time, becoming softer, thinner and more pliable.

Bidding for the best furs

Zilli is also known for its fur. In a room off the third-floor hall are four racks with pelts hanging down either side. Sable, mink, beaver and chinchilla: the quality control is just as rigorous as it is for the leathers next door. Tony Magalhaes, the head of the fur department, goes to auctions in Copenhagen, Toronto, St Petersburg and Milan, bidding for the best in the world. There are about 80,000 chinchilla skins available every year. Less than 8,000 of them are 'black velvet' chinchilla, with a purely black fur. Zilli buys more than half of this production worldwide and uses it for everything from jacket collars to blankets. Many jackets come with interchangeable collars, so you can button on a beaver fur when the temperature requires it. It should be said that Zilli only uses furs from bred animals – all controlled, all breeding pairs. It then operates its own checks to make sure the breeders are sticking to their declared practices.

Tony works downstairs, on the second floor, and has been with Zilli for 37 years. He now works with his son in the same department. Tony's hands are stained black from years of working with the dye they use to colour the skin of the furs. His son, like everyone in the new generation, wears gloves.

RIGHT: The fur room, complete with sable, mink, beaver and chinchilla.

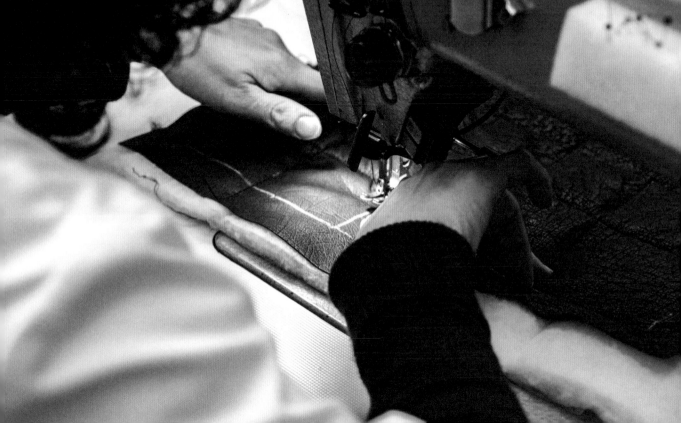

The dyeing procedure is pretty simple, with furs stapled upside down onto a revolving table. The table top turns over, allowing spray guns underneath to cover the backs of the skins, before turning over again. The dye colours the back and seeps through, so no white skin shows at the root of the hairs.

Cut like a suit

Interestingly, the leather jackets are cut in the same way as high-end suits: individually, to cardboard patterns. All clothes used to be made this way until the advent of machinery that cut many layers of cloth at the same time (usually with high-powered water). Cutting by hand takes longer, but it has the advantage that small adjustments can be made quickly and cheaply. This enables jackets to be made to order very easily.

The most common change in a made-to-order jacket is the length of the sleeves. Other, trickier changes are possible, but they often require every leather panel across the jacket to be a little bit wider, which can take time to get right. 'Still, we can normally do a complete order in five or six days if we need to,' says Jean-Michel. 'That's the flexibility of individual construction and an experienced workforce.' Many of the cutters have been at Zilli for 30 or 40 years and each has a specialty: Jean-Claude is the most experienced and tackles hard jobs such as shearling or peccary; Stephanie is particularly skilled at made-to-measure, adjusting the sizes expertly. Each of them cuts an entire jacket from start to finish. The jackets are actually made almost entirely on a sewing machine – the only handwork is around delicate edges, on the pockets and other finishing, and the insertion of some sleeves. Yet the Zilli women, many of whom used to make wedding dresses, are proud of the accuracy of their sewing. At one point some years ago they began putting triple lines of stitching on the jackets. This meant sewing three perfectly straight lines, one after the other, with pinpoint accuracy. Now it has become a Zilli signature: entirely ornamental but indicative of the attention that has gone into a jacket's construction.

TOP AND ABOVE: Paper patterns for the various models of jacket are arranged on a rail.

OPPOSITE AND ABOVE: The patterns are laid out on skins and cut by hand. They then go to the seamstresses to be assembled.

The first luxury leather

Zilli is a relatively modern company – it was founded by Alain Schimel in 1970 after he became fascinated by the leather-work of his family tailor (Teofilo Zilli) and decided to set up an atelier in collaboration with him. Alain was as much an innovator as Alfred Dunhill or Franco Loro Piana. In 1970 the leather jacket was considered worker's clothing, only worn casually by bikers and beatniks. It was not a luxury item and Alain was mocked for his efforts to produce high-end leather garments. This began to change in the 1970s and exploded in the 1980s, with the newly rich snapping up leather coats and their fur accessories. Zilli was the first luxury retailer in Russia, where men took a particular shine to the fur-lined models and bright silk linings. Sales spread across Europe, Central Asia and the Far East and US. In 1996, the company expanded into a broader range of leather goods and pushed the made-to-order programme into accessories and upholstery.

Importantly, Zilli has always remained family-owned. In keeping with its name, it has adopted the Italian tradition of family management, with Alain, his wife and their children, Alexandra, Laurent and Michela, managing everything from jewellery to general development and marketing. This, Alain believes, has enabled it to concentrate on the things it does best, including superlative leather jackets.

ABOVE: Zilli is proud of its history as the first luxury manufacturer of leather jackets, and uses gold and leonine branding throughout the product.

OPPOSITE: The leathers, whether calf, lamb or alligator, are always best appreciated worn, or studied in minute detail.

ZIMMERLI

THE FINEST UNDERWEAR
IN THE WORLD

AN ALPINE PIONEER

A SMALL, SPECIALIST UNDERWEAR
OPERATION IN THE SWISS ALPS,
ZIMMERLI IS DISTINGUISHED
BY THE QUALITY AND VARIETY
OF ITS PRODUCT.

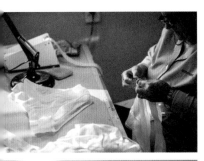

The way the story goes, back in the 19th century Pauline Zimmerli-Bäurlin was widowed, losing her husband soon after they were married. By that time they already had one child together – and many more from her husband's previous marriage. Searching for a way to save money and support the family, Pauline began knitting socks. This was a nice quiet business until one of the sons, Adolf, travelled to England and brought back a knitting machine. No one in Switzerland, and certainly not Pauline, had ever seen one before. But she quickly became a mass manufacturer of socks, selling the delicate product all around Switzerland.

The volume Pauline was selling pales in comparison with the 7,000 pieces a week that Zimmerli produces today. Yet, even at this scale, the modern Zimmerli is one of the most specialized makers of underwear in the world. Compared to the millions of cotton undergarments produced in India and China today, it is still a cottage industry.

A few little places in Switzerland

The main production centre in Coldrerio does not scream luxury. The modest, two-storey building is overshadowed by the Hugo Boss logistics centre next door, which is an imposing metal block set in landscaped grounds. When you walk through the front door of the Zimmerli building, the first thing you see is a picture of the staff: about 50 people in three neat rows, taken in front of the vineyard on the opposite side of the road. The picture is 12 years old. In that time a few people have left – identifiable by the cut-out faces of their replacements that have been glued over the top of them. But only a handful, in a dozen years. This is a close-knit team.

ABOVE AND OPPOSITE: Part of the skill in creating Zimmerli garments is the care required to deal with very delicate cottons, as well as lace.

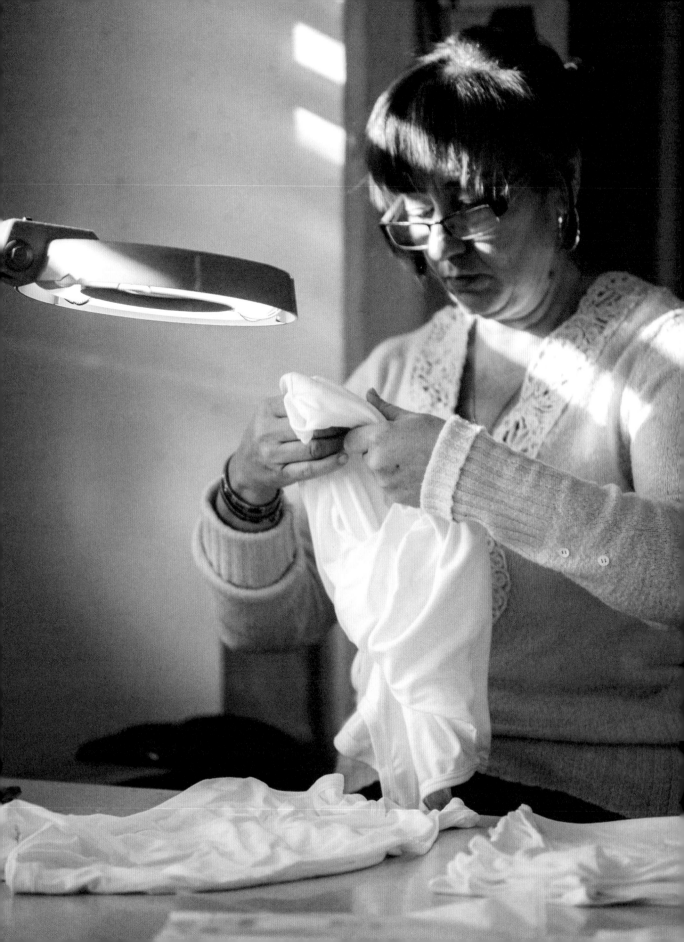

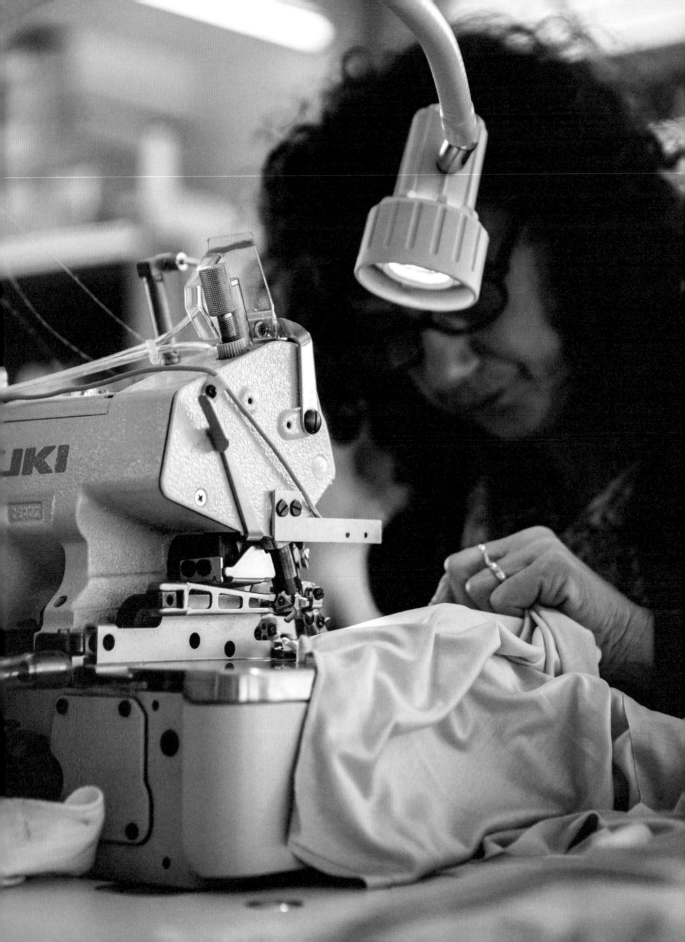

The ground floor is dedicated to quality checking and distribution. Six women are pressing the T-shirts and preparing a Middle Eastern shipment as we enter. An inquiry about who has been at the company longest sparks a few laughs and a good-humoured argument across the pile of boxes in the middle of the floor. Clementina, it turns out, has been at Zimmerli for 40 years. Ivana, working the steam press on the other side of the floor, has been there 39. It will be 40 next year, she assures us. No one has any plans to leave.

Experience is one of the most important aspects to making luxury garments. Quality control is vital and requires knowledge of not just the obvious flaws – stray threads, pulls in the cloth – but the subtle defects that a rote-taught junior might miss. Over 1,000 times every day these women must clip off the excess thread at the edge of every seam and on the back of the Zimmerli label. They must retain the concentration to spot a rare error that only comes up every few hundred pieces.

With the making itself, experience enables seamstresses to jump from one complex piece (say a jersey-knit brief with flat seams) to another (perhaps a delicate silk-mix undershirt). When a new product requires a different way to run the seam – working in greater fullness, for example – then a new method must be developed on an existing machine. For such a small company, Zimmerli produces an astounding range: 1,700 different products.

The stitching, quality control and packing are taken care of here at Coldrerio, in the mountains just across the border from Como in Italy. The panels of cloth are prepared and cut in Mendrisio, just down the road. Aarburg, Pauline's hometown, is where the company headquarters are, although today this is just where the design and marketing are carried out. A small operation in Huttwil houses the old knitting machines that make Zimmerli's signature Richelieu fabric. Much of the cloth is produced in the east of the country,

ABOVE: Quality control, such as removing all stray threads anywhere on a garment, is fundamental to the luxury approach to even simple cotton pieces.

OPPOSITE: The Zimmerli seamstresses have to be able to work on dozens of different materials and designs.

ABOVE AND RIGHT: The edges of the cloth are cut with a saw – it is set up (above) before a chainmail glove is worn (right) to conduct the cutting.

OPPOSITE: One of the tricky aspects of the cutting is getting extremely fine, soft cottons to lie flat at every stage.

where water from the Rhine is used for washing the cotton. This is a Swiss company and it is proud to be the only one making underwear in Switzerland today. Pauline effectively launched the fine knitting industry here – and women like Clementina and Ivana continue it.

The process

Zimmerli doesn't weave its own cloth, so let's start the story of the manufacturing with the moment rolls of material arrive in Mendrisio. Five women work in this small facility and two of them carry a roll up onto the 30-foot-long machine that lays the cloth out in layers, ready to be cut. This machine is 24 years old and was used to cut jeans before Zimmerli bought it. It has a fearsome row of teeth as well as iron gears and an old chain running across it. The skill required, as before, is the ability to spot flaws and to ensure that the cloth is perfectly smooth. The silk-mix material for a new range of nightwear is proving particularly tricky to lay flat, its lightweight surface rippling away from the women's fingers across the broad table.

Once the cloth is ready, paper printouts of the required panels are laid on top. These are sent to a printer in the next room, but the local manager checks them closely to make sure no cloth is wasted. A large, electronic saw roughly cuts up the cloth. The delicate edges are left to a saw on the other side of the room, something that requires a chainmail glove to operate legally. Mendrisio also houses the cloth storage – the men's collection is almost exclusively produced in white and black, but Zimmerli fabrics include Sea Island Cotton, the knitted Richelieu, Egyptian cottons, an elastane mix, silk and wool blends, pure silk jersey, and a micro-modal fibre of which 10,000 metres weigh but a single gram. Womenswear is much more complicated, given the ruffles, synthetic fabrics and lace involved.

The cloth, once cut, is delivered in bundles of the appropriate parts to the seamstresses on the first floor in Coldrerio. There, 30 women take up the jobs of working the dozen or so different seams that go into Zimmerli underwear. The binding on a vest involves a different method (and a more delicate hand) from the waistband of a brief or boxer. Some edges require an undulating action from the worker and precise accuracy to allow the knife underneath the sewing bed to cut off excess. Flat seams use the most complex machine, with seven spools of thread running into a small, overhung needle and bed.

The work is hugely varied, which some women enjoy just as others prefer to do the same job and target efficiency. One woman told us she likes the repeated accuracy required to sew on Zimmerli labels. On the wall above her is a blown-up *Vanity Fair* cover with David Beckham on it: pictures of various models wearing the Richelieu singlets are dotted around the room. The factory is a female environment, and a very social one. My favourite picture in the building is taped to the back of a door: a collage of black-and-white pictures of all the workers when they were children, playing or running about.

ABOVE: The first floor of the Coldrerio facility, and bundles waiting to be worked on.

OPPOSITE: Careful attention is required both to thread the appropriate spools of cotton and to finish the hems and lace.

Why Zimmerli is the best

With some areas of menswear, selecting the best maker in the world is inevitably subjective. But there is really no one to compare with Zimmerli. A few other European companies make very good T-shirts and underwear. The manufacturing process is certainly pretty similar, but Zimmerli stands out because of its ambition: no one else in the world uses the same materials or produces the range of products. If you try them, the two things that strike you are the materials and the variety. The Egyptian and Sea Island Cottons are noticeably softer than any other underwear; they are woven more finely to be almost unnoticeable in their lightness. The thread itself is softer and finer. And the range of possible cottons means you will find your perfect thickness, stretch and style of knit.

The variety is particularly noticeable in the cut of the underwear. One manufacturer in the cotton business told me it took him 30 years to feel confident that he had got the cut of his briefs right. He feels sorry for anyone coming to the industry for the first time and having to design underwear from scratch. With no other piece of clothing is there such little tolerance for discomfort. Zimmerli's Royal Classic line alone has 17 different models. From slips to pants and shorts to boxers, there is a style for every shape. The six different types of Royal Classic slip differ largely in the way the leg is cut away, allowing you to select your preferred angle to within a few degrees. Styles are important for maintaining longevity: a younger customer wants a lower rise and a tighter fit, while older men often prefer a looser boxer or the long 252-842 short, which has a high rise and clean leg reminiscent of the top of 'long johns' or leggings.

The abundance of choice makes Zimmerli a popular brand everywhere, from Japan to Canada, England to Italy. It also means there is consistent appeal across age groups: anyone with the discernment and money to buy the best in the world can find their perfect pant. With a certain modesty and a distinct lack of fuss, Zimmerli is leading the way in underwear production from a little two-storey block in the Swiss Alps. And no one seems to be following.

CARE AND MAINTENANCE

The care and maintenance required for good clothing varies enormously, from the daily washing of shirts to the occasional resoling of shoes. However, where they do need looking after, the attention is often richly rewarded. Suits can last for decades; bags a whole lifetime. The patina that leather goods acquire is often a sufficient reward in itself, never mind the longevity. At the very least, there is little point investing in the finest clothes in the world without some knowledge as to how to maintain them.

Tailoring

The most important aspect of caring for tailoring – whether suit, jacket or coat – is to brush it regularly. Ideally a clothes brush is used at the end of every day to lightly brush down the cloth, removing the day's grime and dust. It is this atmospheric dirt that causes most of the long-term damage.

With that taken care of, tailoring should have to be dry cleaned once a year at most, and only then when there are obvious stains to deal with. It can also be occasionally steamed and pressed, to give life back to the fibres and a crease back to the trousers. Most bespoke tailors provide such a service, as do high-end dry cleaners.

Shirts

Two things usually cause a shirt to age quickly: stains and dry cleaning. Liquid stains need to be dealt with on the spot, dabbing them with a tissue to lift away as much as possible. Water and soap should deal with most others, except for oils. As for stains caused by wear, such as under the armpits and around the collar, putting extra soap on them before a wash is the best course of action. Start early, before the stain is bad, and continue regularly.

Avoid dry cleaning shirts wherever possible. As with all dry cleaning, the chemicals and bulk washing will erode the material more quickly than it would otherwise.

Other cottons

Cottons such as those used in fine underwear, T-shirts or socks should not take much looking after, but it is important to wash them delicately and hang dry. Tumble drying is the most usual cause of shrinkage.

Shoes

Leather shoes require more maintenance than any other item of menswear, but also promise greater rewards. First, a shoe tree should be used at the end of the day when the shoes are removed. This helps absorb moisture lost through the feet, and ensures the upper of the shoe returns to its original shape. Second, shoes should be brushed down at the end of a day's wear. This removes most of the scuffs and bumps and the need to polish frequently.

Polish is there to create a shine on the shoe, rather than cover scuffs. Worked in regularly over years, polish creates a personal patina that is one of the subtlest pleasures in menswear. It can be brushed off after application, but those that care will use a little water and a rag to bring the polish up to a mirror-like shine. We call it spit and polish; the French call it *glaçage*.

Cream should also be used on leather shoes every few months, to feed the leather. And have them resoled and reheeled when required, by the original manufacturer. Do it when the leather is wearing thin, rather than when it has worn through.

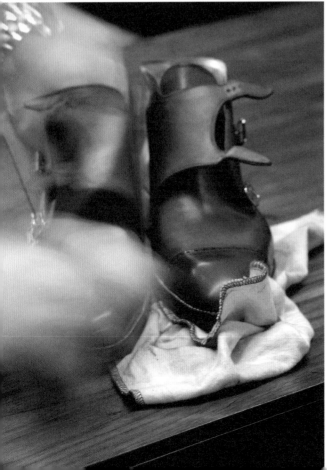

Other leathers

Leather products such as bags and jackets need less attention than shoes, but they both benefit from a little cream or wax now and again – which is best, and in what particular recipe, should be ascertained from the manufacturer. Generally, the thicker the hide of a bag, the waxier a treatment it needs.

Hardware can also benefit from a little care, particularly if it is brass. Some prefer to remove all tarnish with a brass-specific product; others just to clean it with wax.

Ties

A tie should be hung up at the end of the day, in order to allow it to relax and regain its shape. Knitted ties are often rolled in a drawer rather than hung, for fear of them stretching over time (although any effect is minor).

The biggest enemy of the tie is stains, and for this reason it is often worth hiding it when eating – either in the shirt front or flicking it over the shoulder. Many manufacturers do offer a cleaning service, but often the tie must be completely unmade, cleaned and then sewn together again.

Knitwear and scarves

Woollen clothing such as knitwear and scarves should not take much looking after. They should both be washed very occasionally, perhaps once a year. This can normally be done in a delicate cycle on a washing machine. It often helps to put them inside a pillowcase, to prevent stretching. Afterwards roll in a towel to get out most of the moisture, before drying flat on a rack.

Umbrellas

It is always helpful not to furl an umbrella when wet, in case it causes stains down the canopy. And wood benefits from a little oil every now and again.

Jeans

Entire books (or at least blogs) have been written on the best way to wear raw denim. You can wear jeans in the bath; you can freeze them to remove odour; you can wash them once, twice or thrice, to get just the right look, and then never again.

The general advice is to wear raw denim jeans for a good while before washing them – months rather than weeks. This allows them to take on the natural creases caused by the way you wear them. Once they have become too odorous to carry on wearing, wash inside out and pull straight before hanging to dry.

Panama hats

Panama hats should be stored sitting flat, ideally with the front hanging over an edge, such as a shelf. The front naturally rolls downwards, so storing it like this helps retain the shape. During a long summer of wear, a little water can also be sprayed on it once or twice to avoid the straw drying out. Finally, steam is the best solution to any issues with the hat becoming misshapen or even stained.

STOCKISTS

Anderson & Sheppard
www.anderson-sheppard.co.uk
32 Old Burlington Street
London W1S 3AT

Begg & Co.
www.beggandcompany.com
Selfridges
400 Oxford Street
London W1A 1AB

Bergdorf Goodman
754 Fifth Avenue
New York NY 10019

Brent Black
www.brentblack.com

Bresciani
www.brescianisocks.com
www.mrporter.com
www.hangerproject.com

Cifonelli
www.cifonelli.com
32 rue Marbeuf
75008 Paris

GJ Cleverley & Co.
www.gjcleverley.co.uk
13 The Royal Arcade
London W1S 4SL

Drake's
www.drakes-london.com
3 Clifford Street
London W1S 2LF

Alfred Dunhill
www.dunhill.com
Bourdon House
2 Davies Street
London W1K 3DJ

Twin Villas
796 Huai Hai Road
Shanghai

Kapital
www.kapital.jp
www.superdenim.com
www.rawrdenim.com

Kiton
www.kiton.it
14A Clifford Street
London W1S 4JX

4 East 54th Street
New York
NY 10022

11 Via Ges
Milan

Loro Piana
www.loropiana.com
157 New Bond Street
London W1S 2UB

748 Madison Avenue
New York NY 10065

Mario Talarico
www.mariotalarico.it
www.hangerproject.com

Zilli
www.zilli.fr
140 New Bond Street
London W1S 2TW

9–15 Avenue Matignon
75008 Paris

Zimmerli
www.zimmerli.com
366 rue Saint Honoré
75001 Paris

Harrods
87–135 Brompton Road
London SW1X 7XL

Selfridges
400 Oxford Street
London W1A 1AB

Bergdorf Goodman
754 Fifth Avenue
New York NY 10019

Barneys
660 Madison Avenue
New York NY 1006

ACKNOWLEDGMENTS

Many thanks to my family Maria, Lily and Audrey for their support and to photographers Luke Carby and Andy Barnham. Thanks too to the many followers of Permanent Style, and to all the companies included here for their hospitality throughout the research process.